D1476169

Thomas Gilcrease

GILCREASE MUSEUM | TULSA, OKLAHOMA

GILCREASE
MUSEUM

1400 NORTH GILCREASE MUSEUM ROAD

TULSA, OKLAHOMA 74127–2100

Gilcrease Museum is a University of Tulsa/City of Tulsa partnership.

The University of Tulsa is an EEO/AA institution.

©Copyright 2009 by Gilcrease Museum. All rights reserved

International Standard Book Number 978-0-9725657-4-5

Printed in Korea.

SERIES CURATOR: Randy Ramer
ASSOCIATE CURATORS: Carole Klein, Kimberly Roblin
SERIES EDITOR AND DESIGNER: Carol Haralson
PHOTOGRAPHER: Robert S. Cross

Page one: Thomas Gilcrease, ca. 1915

Page two: *Thomas Gilcrease* (detail), 1958. Charles Banks Wilson. 40 x 32, egg tempera/canvas, GM 0127.2300.

Page five: *Turkey Hunter* (detail), 1946. Bert G. Phillips. 39.625 x 25.75, oil/canvas, GM 0137.523.

Gilcrease Museum gallery, early 1950s. Gilcrease Museum.

FACING: *Superstition,* detail, ca. 1921. Ernest L. Blumenschein. 50.25 x 49, oil/canvas, GM 0137.531.

IN A LIFE MARKED BY EXTRAORDINARY HIGHS AND LOWS, Thomas Gilcrease maintained an eye for quality, an appreciation of beauty, and enough personal wealth to create a preeminent collection of western art and Native American material that is today widely recognized as a national treasure.

The collection of the Gilcrease Museum, with more than 12,000 works of fine art, 300,000 ethnographic and archaeological items, and 100,000 rare books and manuscripts, draws thousands of visitors from around the world annually. How the collection was assembled and how the museum came into being is essentially the story of the life and the obsession of one man, Thomas Gilcrease.

Thomas Gilcrease came from humble beginnings. He was born in Robeline, Nachitoches Parish, Louisiana, in 1890, the eldest of an eventual fourteen children born to William and Elizabeth Vowell Gilcrease. The Gilcreases were farmers and millers. William's ancestry was French and Scots-Irish. Elizabeth was one-quarter Muscogee Creek. It was that strain of Indian blood that shaped Thomas's identity and his life. When he was only a few months old, his family moved to the Creek Nation, Indian Territory, where the Dawes Act provided for the division of commonly held Indian land into individual allotments. His one-eighth quantum of Creek blood qualified him for the rolls; he received the enrollment number 1505 and 160 acres of dusty farmland twenty miles south of Tulsa.

Gilcrease's allotment would yield an unforeseen bounty. When wildcatters struck the Glenn Pool in 1905, they uncorked Oklahoma's Oil Boom and newfound wealth for the territory. With some of his first profits, he paid for his education at Bacone College in Muskogee. In 1909, he was persuaded to lease his land for a fraction of its value. Realizing his mistake, he fought the matter in the courts for years, during which time he acquired an excellent education on the technicalities of oil leasing and drilling. He used his knowledge to establish Gilcrease Oil Company in 1922.

His career and his personal life would always bear some mark of struggle. On August 22, 1908, Gilcrease married Belle Harlow, a member of the Osage Nation. The couple had two sons, Thomas, Jr. in 1909 and Barton Eugene in 1911.

In 1912, Gilcrease bought his first work of art, a painting by Ridgeway Knight entitled *Rural Courtship*. He acquired it from a New York art dealer who had set up shop in the Tulsa Hotel and was attracted to it because it was "wholesome."

A short time later, he purchased the house that would become the centerpiece of the current Gilcrease Museum grounds, a native sandstone block house built by Tulsa attorney Flowers Nelson and his wife Carrie, who acquired the property in 1909. Gilcrease liked the stone house and the wraparound porch so well that on December 26, 1913, shortly after construction was completed, he purchased the house, a garage, a barn, and eighty acres from the Nelsons.

In 1924, the sixteen-year marriage between Belle and Thomas ended in divorce, and Thomas rented the house while he traveled abroad buying art in Europe to build his fledgling collection. He hired "Chief" Cephas Stout in 1927 to begin remodeling and updating the rock house property. In 1928, Gilcrease wed nineteen-year-old Norma Smallwood, a Cherokee, shortly after she had completed her reign as the second Miss America. This union would also end in a divorce that played out with some bitterness in the courts. On May 2, 1934, Thomas was awarded the divorce and custody of the couple's five-year-old daughter, Des Cygne Lamour Gilcrease. In 1941, Gilcrease asked Stout to convert the barn and garage into storehouses for his artwork and artifacts. Upon completion, he referred to the barn as his "gallery" and the garage as his "library." The roots of Gilcrease Museum had been planted.

In 1937, Thomas moved Gilcrease Oil Company to San Antonio, Texas, where he continued collecting art. There, six years later, he opened his Museum of the American Indian in the Milam Building. He decided his vacant stone house in Tulsa could be better utilized as an orphanage for Indian children. He made renovations to the second floor, adding more rooms for girls, and built a second building for boys. The garage became a technical training center for the children.

Weak attendance at his San Antonio museum did not deter the avid collector. In 1947, Thomas made the shrewdest acquisition of American art of the 20th century. He purchased the entire collection of the late Dr. Phillip Gillette Cole, an avid New York art collector, for the sum of $250,000. He now owned 636 works by Remington, Russell, Schreyvogel, Seltzer, and other well-known artists.

Thomas Gilcrease, ca. 1940. Billboard for Gilcrease Museum showing one of the museum's most famous paintings, Frederic Remington's *The Stampede*.

FACING: *Breaking Through the Line,* detail. Charles Schreyvogel. 49 x 43, oil/canvas, GM 0127.1235.

Soon sixty-three boxes and eleven crates were delivered to Tulsa. They contained twenty-seven bronzes and forty-six paintings by Charles Russell, seventeen bronzes and twelve paintings by Frederic Remington, and numerous documents and correspondence of well-known historical figures in the American West.

Realizing that he had amassed nothing less than one of the most significant collections in the world in a span of a few decades, Gilcrease hired artist and architect Alexander Hogue to design a museum on his property in which he could display his treasures. In 1949, he opened the Thomas Gilcrease Institute of American History and Art on his rambling estate in Tulsa.

True to the cyclical nature of his life's path and in spite of the fact that Gilcrease had operated on an almost unlimited budget for decades, by the early 1950s he was faced with insurmountable debts. He was forced to seek a buyer for the collection in order to keep it together. Area residents began to realize the loss for Tulsa if the collection were to leave. In a public referendum on August 2, 1954, Tulsans approved by a three-to-one majority a single issue bond of $2.25 million to pay off the debt of a private individual and to take upon themselves the ownership of and responsibility for the collection. Gilcrease committed his personal oil property revenue to the City of Tulsa for assistance in maintaining the museum. In time, the oil revenue equaled the original bond funds and the city's original investment was repaid in full. In 1958, the Gilcrease Foundation conveyed the museum buildings and grounds to the City of Tulsa.

Although Gilcrease had acquired and been surrounded by many priceless treasures, he was sentimental by nature. In the end he aspired to little more than the modest stone home with the wraparound porch and that first "wholesome" painting, which remained on the wall of his living room until his death in 1962. He is buried in a mausoleum on the museum grounds.

Today, the museum's 460 scenic acres, with their botanical gardens and vistas of the Osage Hills, greet visitors with a quiet groundedness, speaking a soft benediction over the turbulent history that gave America one of her greatest repositories of native-born art. Gilcrease Museum houses more than 12,000 paintings, drawings, prints, and sculptures by 400 artists from colonial times to the present, as well as scores of thousands of artifacts, manuscripts, documents, and maps. Each piece widens our window into the discovery, expansion, and settlement of the Americas, with special emphasis on the Old West and the American Indian.

Gilcrease Museum galleries in the early 1950s.

FACING: *The Wild Turkey,* detail, 1845. John James Audubon. 53.25 x 40.5, oil/canvas, GM 0126.2322.

The vision of Thomas Gilcrease was clear. It is not reflected in his writings or speeches, but rather in what he collected and what he did with his collection. He never had a written collections policy or statement of purpose because it was all in his head—and heart. He knew what he liked, and he was willing to go after it. He was

The Vista Room, shown under construction, was part of a major expansion of the museum undertaken in the early 1960s. It was completed shortly after Gilcrease's death.

FACING: *The Grand Canyon of the Yellowstone*, detail, 1872. Thomas Moran. 26.5 x 21.5, watercolor/paper, GM 0226.1619.

a systematic, focused, and meticulous collector. Even in debt, he remained true to the vision of a great museum in Tulsa. His singular devotion to that vision ultimately cost him a great deal, but it purchased even more for future generations who seek to touch the shared history and creative legacy of the American people.

Early Life of Thomas Gilcrease

RANDY RAMER, CURATOR, GILCREASE MUSEUM

Elizabeth Gilcrease (1874–1935), mother of Thomas.

FACING: The family, ca. 1900. William and Elizabeth with Thomas, Edward, Ben, Florence, and Lena. Thomas is at far right behind his father. GM 4326.5456.

BY THE TIME HE WAS FORTY, Thomas Gilcrease had achieved significant wealth as an oil producer and trader. He had been a successful banker, rancher, and farmer. He had been a world traveler. He had married both a schoolgirl and a beauty queen. He had become the father of three children. Even so, the American businessman and entrepreneur remained a man without a clear purpose. His life was marked more by drive than vision. Gilcrease was a man of many temperaments, of extreme passion but also of intense repose. His disposition varied according to circumstance. He could be thoughtful yet thoughtless, possessive but generous. He was often predictable but at the same time could be magically spontaneous. He could be inspiring but also mundane, inquisitive but unwilling to learn from past mistakes. He loved nature and beauty above all things. He pursued life with a fundamental notion that a single human effort could affect the lives of others.

William Thomas Gilcrease was born on February 8, 1890, in Louisiana. His father, William Lee Gilcrease, was an enterprising twenty-two-year-old farmer-merchant whose wife was part Muscogee Creek. The young couple moved to the Creek Nation in Indian Territory within months of their first-born's arrival in order to take advantage of land allotments proposed for members of the Creek Nation. They lived for a time near Twin Mounds. In 1904 the growing family relocated to an area near the Wealaka Mission on the Arkansas River. William Gilcrease founded the town of Wealaka and established a general store there.

Wealaka ca. 1900. GM 4327.1803.
Above, Gilcrease roping cattle.

Thomas Gilcrease was the oldest of fourteen children. In his youth, he learned the value of a hard day's effort. His father expected much from the eldest son. The boy's days began with the tending of livestock and continued with work in the grist mill, cotton gin, or in the family fields as the seasons demanded. The day-to-day work instilled in him a sense of the value of time and labor and forged an industrious temperament that would serve him the remainder of his life. His early years were affected, however, by a birth defect known today as *talipes equinovarus,* or "club foot." While this condition was later corrected by surgery, in childhood it caused the sensitive boy some personal insecurity, particularly in the ongoing effort to perform the daily tasks assigned by his father. The physical handicap also instilled in him an abiding concern for others similarly disadvantaged. In later life, he maintained an interest in helping handicapped and underprivileged children.

Even as a boy, Gilcrease loved to read. He had a natural, insatiable curiosity and an inquisitive mind. Throughout his life, he surrounded himself with books. The written word was as essential as the living air. Newspapers, letters, histories, rare books, and documents would all one day become central to his enduring passion for learning and his appreciation of the past. There is no evidence that young Thomas received regular formal schooling, but he did for a period attend classes taught by the noted Creek writer and poet Alexander Posey in a log cabin schoolroom. It was Posey that instilled in him the value of education and of his Native American heritage. He inspired the boy to pursue the serious quest for knowledge that would ultimately characterize his adult life. In his formative years Thomas Gilcrease

ALEXANDER POSEY

Alexander Posey was born on August 3, 1873 near the town of Eufaula in the Creek Nation. An avid learner from an early age, he attended public school and eventually Bacone Indian University. While there he worked as a librarian and also set type for the school newspaper, *Bacone Indian University Instructor*. It was in this paper in 1892 that he published his first poem, "The Comet's Tale."

Alexander Posey.
GM 4327.6258a.

A youthful Gilcrease on horseback, ca. 1906.

developed an awareness of his place in the world. His Native ancestry eventually became a fundamental point of focus that guided him in his search for a life's purpose.

Gilcrease's early days were a time of opportunity but also of hardship and dramatic cultural change. The close of the American frontier had been declared yet broad swaths of the nation's physical and social landscapes remained raw and undefined. It was on this stage that the boy Gilcrease first began to pursue his own path. Foremost, he was enthralled by the natural world. When not engaged in the daily requirements of his father's going concerns, he made frequent treks though the rural places of Indian Territory. The woods and forests were a school of their own, and their influence would remain with him all the days of his life. Years later, Thomas's longtime friend Robert Lee Humber wrote that "To understand Mr. Gilcrease, one should realize first of all that he was a naturalist, trained from his most tender years in the open spaces of the prairies and in the native haunts of its abundant wildlife. He knew intimately the local habitats of the animals, the songs of birds echoing through forest glens and the rippling music of mountain streams…He was truly a child of the great out-of-doors…"

Throughout his life, the natural elements of the earth energized Thomas Gilcrease with a passion equaled only by his deeply-rooted need to understand its long past. The simple act of looking at plants and animals restored him. In the woods and creek beds of Indian Territory, the boy found a connection to a world

that required from him only a quiet appreciation. Birds and flowers were of particular interest. They inspired in him a keen enthusiasm for the gentle nuances of nature. Later in life, gardens and gardening would become a central interest, whether at the Bois de Boulogne or on the verdant grounds of the Gilcrease estate. As a young man in the still-young wilderness that would soon become the state of Oklahoma, Thomas Gilcrease first developed a profound admiration for the arts of the natural world.

Gilcrease, ca. 1915, exploring a wetland area. His appreciation for the natural world was formed early in his youth. GM 4337.4350. Above, William Gilcrease (1868–1913), father of Thomas.

In the fields and stock pens of the Gilcrease farm, however, the boy worked hard to contribute to the family. Along with his everyday chores, he sometimes sold produce from the back of a wagon, traveling throughout the countryside with strict instructions by his father not to return home until the cart was empty. Thomas Gilcrease's father was, above all things, ambitious. From the time he left Louisiana and throughout the number of homesteads he established across the Indian Territory, he maintained an eye toward opportunity. William Lee Gilcrease was a man driven to succeed. He approached life with an energy and restlessness that was never fully satisfied. The relationship between the boy and the father was likely never particularly close. The elder Gilcrease was a man of short temper who had little patience for idle hands. Thomas Gilcrease friend, biographer, and counsel, David R. Milsten, later wrote about William Lee Gilcrease, "He was a hard man, made so by hard times."

In the early 1900s, the boy's life took a series of turns that would shape him both personally and professionally. In 1899, Thomas Gilcrease had been entered into the tribal rolls of the Creek Nation. When land allotments were dispersed by the federal government, he received 160 acres. By happenstance, his portion of land was located south of the city of Tulsa. In 1905, oil was discovered in the region. Later called the Glenn Pool, the area would become one of the greatest producing oil fields in the history of the United States. At the age of fifteen, Thomas Gilcrease began receiving modest royalties from his holdings. While he did not yet know it, a world of opportunity had opened before him. He was about to take his first steps in a course that he would follow the remainder of his life.

THE GLENN POOL

In the early morning of November 22, 1905, Robert Galbreath and Frank Chelsey struck oil four miles south of Tulsa in the Creek Nation, Indian Territory. Located on the allotment of Ida E. Glenn, a Creek citizen, the oil strike marked a turning point in Tulsa's history. Within a few short days of the discovery, the well was producing over 50 barrels a day, and within two years the famous Glenn Pool was producing 52,000 barrels a day, making the state of Oklahoma the largest producer of oil in the world.

FACING: A map of the Gilcrease oil lease, Glenn Pool. GM 5327.433.

The Gilcrease Lease Glenn Pool. Oklahoma.

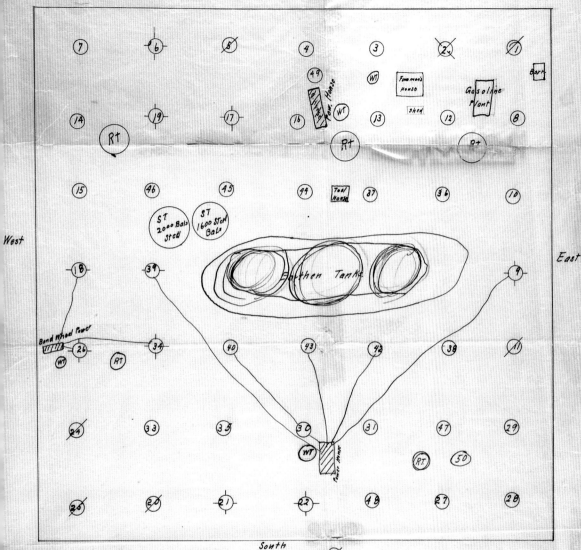

North.

West   East

South

Wells Abandoned Prior to Feb. 8. 1911   ⊘

Wells Abandoned Since. Feb. 8. 1911 ------ ⊗

Wells Claimed as Exhausted Feb. 1911 ------ ⊕

Receiving Tanks ---------------- (Rt) Large 250 Bals Small 50 Bals.

South Power House Operates on South 80 Acres including 9 + 39.

Wells 18. 26. 34 Operated by Band Wheel Power.

North Power House Operates all Wells on North 80 Acres.

FACING: The Nora Brown lease. Inset, the Salazar B-2 gushing oil.

Gilcrease and his brother-in-law Pete Akers in 1906 (GM 4327.3068), bottom, and the two friends in 1908.

The young man knew that education was essential to his ambitions, even as he remained uncertain about the nature of those goals. He enrolled at Bacone College in Muskogee, Oklahoma. School would soon lead to other distractions. In September of 1907, Thomas Gilcrease first met Belle Harlow on the train between Tulsa and Muskogee. He was immediately captivated and pursued her affections with a resoluteness that would characterize much of his adult life. Over the next several months, the two made every effort to spend time together, often touring the scenic

countryside by horse and buggy. The eighteen-year-old Gilcrease's mind remained set. He confided in his good friend (and Belle's brother-in-law) Pete Akers that he was determined to marry the fifteen-year-old. Indeed, Thomas and Belle were married only months later on August 22, 1908.

The newlyweds lived in Wealaka with Gilcrease's parents, then moved to a farm north of Tulsa. Their early years together were a time of considerable happiness. The couple welcomed the birth of their first child, Thomas Gilcrease, Jr. on July 23, 1909. For Thomas Gilcrease, business interests continued to expand as well. He had inherited his father's entrepreneurial spirit and soon found himself pursuing the oil business with a seriousness of mind that would become highly respected by

Belle Harlow, 1908. GM 4327.3060.
Below, Thomas as a young man.

BELLE HARLOW

Born to Warren and Susan Harlow in 1893, Belle Harlow was an enrolled citizen of the Osage Nation. Education was highly valued in the Harlow family and Belle attended Sacred Heart College and Bacone College. It was on a train to Bacone that she met a fellow student, Thomas Gilcrease. After the couple's fourteen-year marriage ended in divorce, Belle lived in Long Beach, California, with her two sons, and later in San Antonio, Texas.

his competitors. In the coming years, he would discover that he had a demeanor well suited to business matters. Just as important to his success, however, would be the knack he developed for finding oil. Yet as his business pursuits and successes increased, his home life began to deteriorate. Young Thomas Gilcrease had entered a world of high competition that was largely dominated by older, more experienced men. It was a world that required instinct but also tenacity of character. Only a few years into marriage, Belle found herself engaged in a competition as well—with her husband's commercial interests and driving ambition.

Above, Gilcrease with his sons Thomas Jr. and Barton, 1915. GM 4337.7831. Immediate right, Barton Gilcrease (1911–1991); far right, Thomas Gilcrease Jr. (1909–1967). Both studio portraits made ca. 1915.

Nine months pregnant with her second child, Belle Harlow Gilcrease filed for divorce in Tulsa County District Court. The case was dismissed, however, on the same day after she and Thomas came to an agreement. Just over a week later, on April 12, 1911, Belle gave birth to a son, Eugene Barton. In 1913, the family moved to a stone house on property at the southern end of the Osage Nation that would one day be referred to as the Gilcrease Estate. Throughout the next decade, as their sons grew from infants into young boys, Thomas and Belle's married life continued to erode. In the early 1920s, the family moved to San Diego where Gilcrease was expanding his business interests. The change in location did little, however, to change the climate of his marriage. The couple continued to grow apart.

In early 1922, Thomas established Gilcrease Oil Company. That same year, after nearly a decade and a half, his marriage was fundamentally over. Gilcrease moved out of the home and into a place of his own in Long Beach, California.

Despite his marital troubles, Thomas Gilcrease remained a man with a relentless energy for life. He enjoyed the outdoors, particularly hunting and fishing. He had acquired a cabin and a stretch of land along the Snake River near the Grand Tetons in Wyoming that would become his personal retreat for decades. In late August of 1924, Gilcrease went on a month-long hunting trip to Alaska. He chronicled the events of his travels in an article he wrote for *Outdoor Life* magazine titled "Fires and Misfires on the Kenai Peninsula." During the hunt, Gilcrease encountered a mother bear and her cubs. With little thought of the consequences, he aimed his rifle and shot the mother bear, which caused the cubs to scramble crying for the safety of the woods. The killing of the mother bear remained in his thoughts for many years. Hunting had lost its luster. Shortly after his return from Alaska, Belle again filed for divorce. Despite

the disappointments and frustrations of their relationship, the two remained friendly toward each other for the rest of their lives.

Thomas Gilcrease eventually returned from California to his Tulsa office. Moving about from place to place had become not only a pleasure but was often a necessity. Regardless, the stone house in the Osage Hills would always remain his home ground. In 1927, Gilcrease was at a high point in his career. The thirty-seven-year-old oilman was poised for new challenges at levels both professional and personal. At a social gathering in Tulsa, he was introduced to Norma Des Cygne Smallwood, the eighteen-year-old Oklahoman from Bristow who was crowned Miss America of 1926. Norma Smallwood was a celebrity unlike any other in the state. Her beauty and charm were keenly documented in newspapers across the nation. She was courted by Hollywood and Madison Avenue alike. Thomas Gilcrease was immediately smitten. Again with

FACING and above, Gilcrease the avid hunter. With pronghorn antelope, left, in 1915, and with a moose in Alaska, ca. 1924. GM 4317.7876. FACING, far left, Gilcrease in Alaska, ca. 1924. GM 4317.3096.
Cover of the issue of *Outdoor Life* for which Gilcrease wrote.

Norma Smallwood, center, Miss America. GM 4327.6053.

characteristic determination of thought and purpose, he set out to win her affections. The two were married the following year.

The relationship between Thomas and Norma Gilcrease was from the onset complex, made more so by the birth of their daughter Des Cygne Lamour Gilcrease in June of 1929. Gilcrease's intensely active business and travel interests conflicted with married life from the very beginning. He was becoming more and more possessive of his young wife as well, complicated by their increasing time and distance apart. For a while, the small family lived in Paris. Gilcrease had expanded his business there but also wanted to expose his young wife to a world beyond the United States. Eventually the marriage of Thomas and Norma Gilcrease ended, but not without considerable acrimony. Despite the hostility, their daughter was loved equally by both parents. Des Cygne would always hold a special place in her father's heart.

Norma Smallwood. Clockwise from far left, posing in a gown; in her riding costume; in a portrait shot; on her horse; in a bathing suit. GM 4327.6053.

FACING: Thomas Gilcrease with his daughter Des Cygne Gilcrease, ca. 1937. GM 4327.6541.

Below, father and daughter in 1933.

By the early 1930s, the course of Thomas Gilcrease's life seemed set. His business prospects seemed boundless. Though he had married twice unsuccessfully, he had also become the father of three wonderful children. He had traveled the world and developed an awareness of its diverse histories and cultures. He had made millions in financial markets around the globe. Still he was not satisfied. Increasingly, business was becoming merely a means to an end. For all of his vast accomplishments, he was a man waiting impatiently for his life's meaning to reveal itself.

Thomas Gilcrease and His Pursuit

KIMBERLY ROBLIN, ASSOCIATE CURATOR, GILCREASE MUSEUM

FACING: The building known as the Casino Club in San Antonio became the Gilcrease Building in 1941. Top, the library in 1943; bottom, an interior gallery with *Contested Game* on view at the end of the corridor; below, the building's exterior.

Right, *Buffalo Crossing the Missouri River*. William de la Montagne Cary. 11.875 x 23.625, oil/canvas, GM 0126.1851.

ON MARCH 18, 1943, Thomas Gilcrease opened his museum to the public, fulfilling an idea first conceived twelve years earlier in a Paris hotel. Located on the sixth floor of the Gilcrease Building in San Antonio, Texas, the museum displayed an impressive and expansive collection that primarily illustrated scenes and themes from American history. Works by Frederic Remington, George Catlin, Albert Bierstadt, William de la Montagne Cary, and others represented one era in particular—the American West. Rugged and compelling, it inspired these and other artists to commit to canvas the dramatic images it conjured. They were scenes not unfamiliar to Gilcrease because defined within this legacy was Oklahoma, the land of his youth. While many claim the influence of place on their lives, Gilcrease could resolutely state that Oklahoma had literally and figuratively shaped his life, propelling him to this Thursday afternoon. Indeed, the parallels between the development of Thomas Gilcrease and Oklahoma were remarkable. At fifty-three, he held many titles—successful and respected businessman, millionaire, father, friend. Through characteristic perseverance he had now gained another—museum founder. But why had he sought this title? When and why did he begin collecting art and decide to establish a museum? There are no simple answers, but an examination of his early life provides insight into his motivations. As a student of history, Gilcrease viewed the past as prologue. We must examine his past then, and begin at the beginning in the rural countryside of the Creek Nation, Indian Territory.

THE EDUCATION OF THOMAS GILCREASE

The childhood of Thomas Gilcrease differed little from that of most children in northeastern Indian Territory. Thomas's father farmed and Thomas and his siblings helped when needed. While the Gilcrease family valued education, the necessities of work held a strong claim on them, and young Thomas's formal education was inconsistent. Some years he did not attend school at all. First impressions are often the most important, however, and Gilcrease once recollected: "I started to school in a one-room log cabin which was conducted by Alex Posey, the Creek poet. He was intelligent, had a keen insight into people and all things around him. I was the first student of Alex on the first day he taught and it was in his father's log cabin that the school was founded. I will always hold him in my memory as a kindly and helpful man and hope that I have in some measure followed in his ways."

It was through Posey that young Thomas learned about Andrew Jackson and the forced removal of Indian tribes from their native homelands, and as a result he began to understand the power of historical events. An appreciation for history was part of his larger and passionate interest in many areas of learning. From youth he loved to learn and perhaps it was his years spent in the fields instead of school that drove his self-education. He understood early that the process of education was not confined to the four walls of a one-room schoolhouse but could occur anywhere at any time. As he grew older he maintained this philosophy, learning from his travels across the country and abroad, in museums and galleries, and in conversations with friends and business associates. Every situation offered an opportunity to learn. He always valued formal education, however, and at seventeen he briefly attended Bacone Indian College. On a train to school one day he met Belle Harlow, a young Osage student. The two soon married. But his life was changing dramatically in other ways as well.

Gilcrease examining a well, ca. 1920.

Gilcrease with Red Branscum, immediately above, in 1925. Branscum began by working for Gilcrease in his oil fields and eventually became vice-president and superintendent of Gilcrease Oil Company.

MR. GILCREASE GOES TO TULSA

Born in 1890, Thomas Gilcrease came of age at roughly the same time that Indian Territory did. As it became the forty sixth state in the Union in 1907, Thomas was transitioning from adolescence to adulthood. Nowhere was Oklahoma's transition more apparent than in the nearby city of Tulsa, once a small Creek settlement and now the capital of the newly developing oil industry. As people had once migrated to California during the Gold Rush, they now came to Tulsa for the new gold, the black gold—oil. Gilcrease was no exception when he and his young bride moved to the city in 1908. Unlike many, however, he already claimed a substantial and profitable stake in the industry. As a citizen of the Creek Nation he had received a 160-acre allotment near Kiefer that was fortuitously located within the famous Glenn Pool. Only a minor when the oil was discovered, he could not legally manage the land. His father acted on his behalf and in 1906 leased the allotment to William H. Milliken under a contract that stipulated a $17,000 bonus and one-eighth royalties from any oil and gas production. Three years later, in August 1909, forty-nine wells on the land were producing 25,000 barrels of oil each month. With royalties streaming in and legally of age, Thomas assumed management of his financial and business affairs.

He brought to Tulsa his passion for knowledge and his new wife. In a short time, Thomas had gone from country boy to business manager and husband. It was an adjustment to be sure, but he thrived in the business world. Not content to be less than directly and wholly involved, he studied geology and oil lease regulations, wanting to be educated on affairs directly affecting his business. He spent a great deal of time in the oil fields, preferring to be present when new wells "blew in," telegraphing his friends when they "roared."

The young husband and wife became parents to Thomas Jr. in 1909 and Barton in 1911. The following year another first occurred when Thomas bought his first piece of art. The large oil painting called *Rural Courtship* perhaps reminded Gilcrease of his own with Belle. Throughout his collecting career, he maintained particular affection for this first piece. Although he did not purchase much art while in his twenties, he did pursue his love of art through learning. He and Belle traveled the country, from the 1915 World's Fair in San Francisco to New York City, stopping at museums and galleries at every opportunity. His travels, however, were not limited

only to cities. He also spent a great deal of time near Jackson Hole, Wyoming, and in the Alaskan wilderness on the Kenai Peninsula. He was young, increasingly successful, and already demonstrating a characteristic that lasted throughout his life. Prescribing to Lord Byron's dictum, Gilcrease took all learning to be his province. Whether it was experiencing a new city, camping in the wilderness, or visiting a museum, he firmly believed in the pursuit of knowledge. In his twenties, he followed his curiosity from Oklahoma to the streets of New York City. In the 1920s, however, the pursuit would take him even further.

THE OKLAHOMAN ABROAD

If the first decade of the 20th century was marked by exploration and extreme growth for Thomas Gilcrease, the second decade was a time of beginnings and ends. By the 1920s, the oil industry in Tulsa was officially booming and Gilcrease's oil and gas leases had grown considerably. In an effort to increase organization and efficiency, he formed Gilcrease Oil Company in 1922 with $100,000. Acting as president, he chose men he knew and trusted as his officers: F. G. Walling and W. Z. Dozier as vice presidents, Pierce Larkin as treasurer, G. B. Bancroft as secretary, and C. H. Steel as assistant secretary. His career as an oilman was thriving. His personal life, unfortunately, was suffering and in 1924 his marriage to Belle ended in divorce. The following year, perhaps to take his mind from recent troubles, he decided to travel abroad. While probably not his first trip overseas, this journey made a lasting impression on him and influenced his collecting and vision for his later museum. Sparing no expense, he sailed on the *Leviathan,* at the time the largest and most luxurious ocean liner. He arrived in France in November 1925 where he rendezvoused with Nema Bouttier, a French businessman and acquaintance. On November 30 the two set out from Nice to spend four and a half months exploring the history and scenery of the Mediterranean. A journal kept by Mr. Bouttier recorded their travels and excursions.

Marseilles, the ancient port city on the French Riviera, was their first stop. Two weeks later they had visited Algiers, Biskra, Tunis, Batna, and Constantine. They had also stopped at Timgad, the ancient Roman settlement founded by Emperor Trajan, and Carthage, the birthplace of the infamous Roman antagonist, Hannibal. The end of December saw them in Rome, where they spent Christmas day at St. Peter's Basilica. In the following days they toured the Vatican and Gilcrease spent considerable time among the 230,000 volumes of the Vatican archives. They visited the Forum, the Arch of Titus, the Circus Maximus, the catacombs, the tombs of Keats and Shelley, and the Villa Borghese where they saw works by Titian, Rafael, and Michelangelo.

UNITED STATES LINES

S. S. "LEVIATHAN," WORLD'S LARGEST SHIP

Thomas Gilcrease booked passage on the *S. S. Leviathan* in late 1925.

FACING: *Rural Courtship,* ca. 1840. Ridgeway Knight. oil/canvas, 26 x 21.875, GM 0126.2352.

Rural Courtship was the first painting acquired by Gilcrease. He kept it with him all his life.

THE GRAND TOUR

When Gilcrease embarked on his nearly five-month tour abroad in November of 1925, he was following in the tradition of the Grand Tour, a custom established in the 17th century in which privileged men and sometimes whole families made leisurely journeys across the Continent. Just as Gilcrease did, they focused on sites of historic and cultural value such as Athens and Rome. Gilcrease took in the sights and history of France, Italy, Algeria, Greece, and Turkey.

Clockwise from facing left, the Hotel Transatlantique in Algiers; in Egypt; in Athens; seaside near an early-day automobile; with a young woman in a field.

In January, they sailed for Egypt, where they stayed nearly a month. The two visited Port Said, Luxor, Karnak, Assuan, Memphis, Alexandria, and Cairo, taking in the pyramids, the Great Sphinx, and the temples. From there they journeyed to Jerusalem, Bethlehem, Haifa, Athens, and Constantinople, passing through the gateway to the Near East, the Dardanelles. In Jerusalem they visited Golgotha and the Church of the Holy Sepulcher. In Athens they toured the Acropolis and walked the streets that gave rise to modern democracy.

By March they had returned to Italy, visiting Florence and Venice. In Venice, "the Renaissance seemed to come alive before them in the cobbled streets and bridged canals." Although not mentioned specifically, they would have also visited St. Mark's Basilica and the Doge's Palace. After almost five months, Gilcrease sailed for home. While it is impossible to quantify the precise effects of this trip, it is possible to discern its tremendous influence. Touring the ancient world fueled his thirst for knowledge and expanded his view of the world.

Thomas Gilcrease, ca. 1915. GM 4327. 7826 (top) and GM 4327. 4349 (bottom).

Norma Smallwood, top, and Gilcrease (shown ca. 1920) began their life together in 1928. Right, Thomas Gilcrease in the Black Mountains of France, ca. 1930. GM 4327.7825.

Over the next five years, Thomas's business and personal wealth continued to grow, and in 1927 his personal life expanded as well when he met and fell in love with a beautiful young Oklahoman crowned Miss America the previous year. The courtship was brief; in September 1928 the two married. The following year they welcomed their daughter, Des Cygne, and shortly after her birth, the family traveled to Paris and took up residence in an apartment on the Rue de Camerons. It was in Paris that Gilcrease forged a friendship that would directly influence the formation and vision of his foundation and museum.

AN AMERICAN IN PARIS

Six months after their arrival, Gilcrease met a young academic who would play a pivotal role in the development and conceptualization of his museum. Robert Lee Humber, a North Carolina native, was a Rhodes scholar, a graduate of both Oxford and Harvard, and a veteran of the first World War. He had taken a position at the American University Union in Paris, an institution that fostered intellectual discussions between American students and professors. The purpose of the organization had expanded to include European and American businessmen living in Europe. Gilcrease, always a student of history, took an interest in the organization, and it was there that he met Robert Humber. Their relationship would span two decades.

A little over a year into the two men's friendship, Gilcrease revealed to Humber his vision for the future. Humber was familiar with the intellectual and philosophical inclinations of his friend as the two had spent many afternoons deep in conversation in tearooms and gardens across Paris. It was in a hotel lobby, however, that Gilcrease revealed his latest subject of contemplation, his vision for the future. No one can say with any certainty when Gilcrease began to contemplate how he could best use his money to "leave a track" for future generations. Perhaps as a young man he determined to use his fortune for good. Perhaps it was in touring the Mediterranean that he began pondering the possibility of a museum. Somewhere, during some time, he formulated a concept for how he would use his good fortune. While in the lobby of the Hotel Lutetia, Gilcrease told Humber he wanted to establish a Gilcrease Foundation that would fund a museum, a library, and a home for underprivileged children. Trusting the skill and intellect of his friend, he asked Humber to draft the charter for his foundation. It should have come as no surprise to Humber that Thomas Gilcrease, a lover of education, wanted to use his money to educate and inform others.

Since his purchase of *Rural Courtship* nineteen years earlier, Gilcrease had continued collecting art, particularly over the past year. To open a museum, however, he would need a larger and more concentrated collection. He originally envisioned a museum similar to most found in the United States and Europe—one that housed a collection of primarily European art. After discussing his idea with Humber, however, he realized there was an opportunity to create a museum with a unique focus—the art of the American West. The market for European art was highly competitive and offered a restricted opportunity for Gilcrease to amass a substantial collection, but art of the American West was little sought after.

With a plan for the future, Gilcrease dedicated the rest of the 1930s to developing his art collection and expanding his business pursuits. In 1933, after receiving considerable interest from European counterparts, Gilcrease organized a French subsidiary of Gilcrease Oil Company. He appointed his friend Robert Humber as director. The branch operated from an office located on the fashionable Champs Élysées. Four years later, further business changes came stateside when restrictive Oklahoma business laws prompted Gilcrease to move his company to San

FACING: Gilcrease and Humber. Above, Humber and an unidentified man, Paris, ca. 1934. GM 4327.7827.

Gilcrease and Humber, at right, at the Gilcrease Oil offices in Paris, Champs-Élysées, ca. 1934. GM 4327.7827.

Antonio, Texas. He made several trips across the Atlantic during the 1930s, attending to business affairs and collecting art. Unfortunately, while his business prospered, his personal life once again declined. His second marriage, like his first, ended in divorce. Consumed with collecting, he focused his energies on art and business.

Buying in the United States and Europe, in single acquisitions and gathered collections, he pursued his goal. He hired an art dealer to help locate pieces for sale and at auction and even purchased an airplane for frequent trips across the Atlantic. He collected not only paintings but also archival materials, including many rare books, maps, and atlases he found in Europe. Correspondence from European dealers, mostly from Belgium, reveals a hint of the amount of art he purchased while in Europe during the late 1930s. Although the letters did not identify pieces by name, they often recorded the number of items to be crated and shipped transatlantic.

Right, *The Bronco Buster,*
1909. Frederic Remington.
32.375 x 16.25 x 30, bronze,
GM 0827.34.

Left, Gilcrease Museum in
San Antonio, ca. 1943, with
Cary's *Return of the Northern
Boundary Survey* visible at the
end of the corridor.

OVERLEAF: *Return of the
Northern Boundary Survey.*
William de la Montagne Cary.
44 x 84, oil/canvas,
GM 0126.2024.

A CULMINATION

By 1940, Gilcrease was nearing the realization of his vision. His commitment was evidenced by the large and impressive collection he now owned. Records from the early 1940s illustrate two of his collecting characteristics. He often purchased several pieces at a time and he favored particular art dealers and galleries, such as the Kennedy Galleries of New York. He was a familiar figure to art dealers both in the United States and abroad. From 1940 through 1942, he purchased several pieces including *Blockhouse* by E. C. Coates, *Battle of Monitor and Merrimac* by John A.

The Herd. Frank Reaugh. 13.5 x 34.75, pastel/paper, GM 1327.1281.

The Cheyenne, 1901. Frederic Remington. 22.25 x 7.125 x 23.5, bronze, GM 0827.40.

Shaumonekupsse (Prairie Wolf),
1825. Charles Bird King.
19 x 15.25, oil/wood,
GM 0126.2221.

Rent-Che-Was-Me, (Female Flying Pigeon), 1825. Charles Bird King.
21.758 x 18.252, oil/wood, GM 0126.1202.

George Washington.
Rembrandt Peale. 37 x 32.5,
oil/canvas, GM 0126.1005.

Knight, *The Waning Moon* and *Summertime* by Frank Reaugh, *Lake George* by Homer Dodge Martin, *The Doll* by Seth Eastman Johnson, four pieces by Albert Bierstadt, *Penn's Treaty* by Edward Hicks, *Indians with Pilgrims* by Henry Bruckner, and *George Washington* by Rembrandt Peale. This small sampling illustrates the breadth of his desire to collect western art, and in essence by doing so to "collect" American history.

He was becoming closer to executing his plan. In 1942, the Thomas Gilcrease Foundation was formed, a first and formal step in the realization of his idea. Its charter clearly formulated the mission of the foundation: "to establish, maintain, and support any educational, scientific, historical, or literary undertaking by means of collecting, assorting, classifying, and exhibiting antiques, relics, objects, and specimens having scientific, historical, cultural, or educational value of this or past periods. . . ."

In 1943, after twelve years of dedicated collecting, he opened his museum and library. Five hundred miles from his childhood home in Oklahoma, his museum in San Antonio represented a much longer passage. He had traveled far from the young boy to the sophisticated oilman he now was, every experience from youth to maturity having helped to shape and define his character. The man who loved education, who believed the pursuit of knowledge should never end, used his fortune to help others learn. His classroom was not one of chalkboards and desks, but of paintings and documents, a place where history became more than a word and the past came alive. Like Alexander Posey, the Creek poet he so admired, Thomas Gilcrease had become a teacher.

OVER FORTY YEARS Thomas Gilcrease put together an outstanding collection that in 1955 became the Thomas Gilcrease Institute of American History and Art. A decade earlier Gilcrease had quietly made a brilliant purchase that added hundreds of paintings and sculpture to his growing art collection, including masterpieces by Western artists Charles M. Russell and Frederic Remington.

In 1944, two years after Gilcrease had incorporated the Thomas Gilcrease Foundation and a year after he opened his first museum to the public in San Antonio, Texas, he purchased the estate collection of Dr. Philip Cole. Prior to this, the Gilcrease collection included none of the Western art for which it is so well known today.

  Thomas Gilcrease's acquisition of Philip Cole's collection is now legendary among Western art aficionados. The fabulous triumph added what are arguably the most beloved art treasures to Thomas Gilcrease's great museum, pieces such as

FACING: Interior of the Cole Estate, New York. GM 4327.6.

Above right, *Breaking Through the Line.* Charles Schreyvogel. 49 x 43, oil/canvas, GM 0127.1235.

Russell's *Meat's Not Meat Till It's In the Pan,* Frederic Remington's *The Stampede,* and Charles Schreyvogel's *Breaking Through the Line.*

Philip Cole was born in Illinois in 1883 and raised in Montana on his father's cattle ranch. He attended Princeton University, graduating in 1906, then Columbia Medical School. After his internship, he returned to Montana to practice medicine in Helena. Called to service during World War I as a reserve medical officer in France, Cole did not return to his practice in Montana after the war ended, but moved to New York. His father, Charles K. Cole, offered him a lucrative partnership in his auto parts manufacturing company, located in Brooklyn. Philip Cole served as president of the company after his father's death in 1920 before retiring in 1930.

The Cole estate, below, and Dr. Philip G. Cole and wife, 1937. GM 4327.1945.

Missing Montana, Philip Cole began in 1919 to purchase paintings, sculpture, photographs and books that reminded him of the West. Working with dealers and directly with artists, he became a highly discerning collector, selecting some of the finest works available. But he kept a very low profile, as is often the hallmark of a private collector; few of the works he owned were ever seen or known outside his family home. One rare exception was a series of memorial exhibitions in California and New York after Charles Russell died, to which Cole sent a few of his paintings—as an anonymous lender, of course.

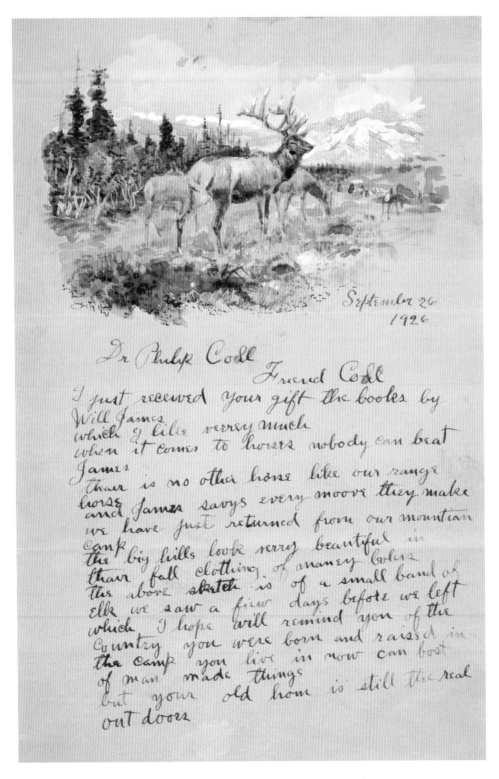

COLE AND RUSSELL

Cole's first Russell painting, *The Buffalo Hunt* (1900), was given to him by his father as a wedding present in 1913. The last one Cole acquired was *Lewis and Clark Expedition,* just before his death in 1941. In between the two, Cole purchased more than seventy other paintings and sculptures by Russell, most directly from Russell's wife and agent, Nancy. The acquisitions began in 1925 and continued for many years after Russell's death. Both Philip Cole and Nancy Russell were determined to get the best possible deal, which resulted in spirited correspondence and tough negotiation. In one of their first business encounters, Cole commissioned a scene of the discovery of gold in Helena, Montana, called *Pay Dirt* (1925), one of the last oils Russell painted. Cole also received the last illustrated letter Russell wrote, dated September 26, 1926, barely a month before the artist died.

Illustrated letter to Philip Cole from Charles Marion Russell, dated September 26, 1926. GM 0237.1583.

and when it coms to making the beautiful
Ma nature has man beat all ways from
the ace
and that old lady still owns a lot of
montana
to show what I mean man made this
animal   but the old lady Im
talking   about made this one

I have made a living painting
pictures of the horned ox and
the life about him   it took regular men
to handle real cows
I would starve to death painting the hornles
deformity
God made cows with horns to defend herself
and when a wolf got meat it wasent easy
often he was so full of horn holes he wasent
hungry
a weasel could kill the man one with out
getting a scrach
but I forgot Iv got no kick coming Iv
been turned my self
but the medicine men at Rochester
ouely took from me things I dident need
and was glad to get rid of   but Im still verry
weak   I look and feel better
if you   see Olaf Seltzer give him my
regards
I suppose by this time hes a real New Yorker
we have been having lots of snow but to day
it has cleard and I think the storm is over
we all send our best regards to you and
yours
        your friend
                    C M Russell

Meat's Not Meat 'Till It's in the Pan,
1915. Charles Marion Russell.
23 x 35, oil/canvas, GM 0137.2244.

Pay Dirt, 1925. Charles Marion
Russell. 24.125 x 35.875, oil/canvas,
GM 0137.901.

Lewis and Clark Expedition,
1918. Charles Marion Russell.
36.75 x 54.75, oil/canvas,
GM 0137.2267.

The Buffalo Hunt, 1900.
Charles Marion Russell.
47.5 x 70.75, oil/canvas,
GM 0137.2243.

OVERLEAF: *The Pony Express,*
1924. Frank Tenney Johnson.
48 x 62.25, oil/canvas,
GM 0127.1088

COLE AND REMINGTON

By the time Cole began collecting in 1919, Frederic Remington had been dead for a decade. At the time of his death, Remington's work was receiving good reviews and his sales were brisk. But after his death, with no new work coming before the critics, interest waned. However, during Cole's active collecting years, Remington's work was again actively sought. The paintings Cole was able to acquire represent a mixed bag, but among them are masterpieces such as *The Stampede* and *Indian Warfare,* both painted at the height of Remington's ability. More remarkable, though, is the collection of bronzes that Cole accumulated, seventeen of the twenty-two subjects that Remington completed. Including the one-of-a-kind *Buffalo Horse,* the rare *Coming Through the Rye, The Norther,* of which only four were cast, and Remington's final piece, *The Stampede,* the Cole collection of bronzes is the most complete of any in the world.

Interior of Cole Estate, New York. GM 4327.6.

The Stampede, 1908. Frederic
Remington. 26.5 x 39.625,
oil/canvas, GM 0127.2329.

OVERLEAF: *Indian Warfare,* detail,
1908. Frederic Remington. 37 x 58,
oil/canvas, GM 0127.2307.

Buffalo Horse, 1907. Frederic Remington. 35.75 x 12, bronze, GM 0827.51.

FACING: *Coming Through the Rye,* 1902. Frederic Remington. 29.5 x 30.5 x 30, bronze, GM 0827.42.

COLE AND SELTZER

Olaf Seltzer met Philip Cole in 1926 through mutual friend Dr. W. T. Butler in Helena, Montana. Cole assumed the role of patron to Seltzer, buying individual paintings such as the masterpiece *Prowlers of the Prairie* and commissioning several series of historical works. Collaborating with Cole on ideas, Seltzer painted "Western Characters," seventy-nine watercolors representing the types of men and women one might have encountered in the West. Upon completion, Seltzer began work on a group of 110 miniature oils that illustrated important historical events of the 19th century, called "Montana in Miniature." Although Seltzer spent a short period of time painting at Zeeview, most of the work was done at home in Great Falls, Montana. Artist and patron kept in touch, Seltzer sending Cole illustrated letters that detailed subjects and compositions. Seltzer's letters were prized as works of art, framed and displayed by Cole.

Letter to Cole from Seltzer, January 23, 1931. GM 0237.1177.
Interior of Cole Estate, New York. GM 4327.6.

COLE COLLECTION STATISTICS

Included among the more than 600 oils, watercolors, and bronzes are: 149 oils and 90 watercolors by Olaf C. Seltzer; 68 oils by Joseph H. Sharp; 29 oils, 16 watercolors and 27 bronzes by Charles M. Russell; 12 oils and 17 bronzes by Frederic Remington; 9 oils and 3 watercolors by Frank Tenney Johnson; 8 oils by Charles Schreyvogel.

The Cole Estate, New York. GM 4327.6.

At the time of his death in 1941, Cole had amassed more than 600 paintings and sculptures, all of which he kept at his estate, Zeeview, in Tarrytown, New York. A list of the artists represents the canon of early 20th-century American Western art. In addition to Russell and Remington are Joseph Henry Sharp, Olaf C. Seltzer, Frank Tenney Johnson, William R. Leigh, Charles Schreyvogel, Will James, Oscar Berninghaus, Edward Borein, W. Herbert Dunton, James Earle Fraser, A. P. Proctor, and N. C. Wyeth.

After Cole's death, his widow, working with the estate's trustees, decided to sell his collection. Knowing Mrs. Cole's desire to keep it intact, New York dealer Daniel Brown, who handled the sale, looked for a buyer who would be able to buy the entire collection. Brown made Thomas Gilcrease aware of its availability. Gilcrease visited New York in 1943 to see the collection and determined that it suited both his personal tastes and his plans for expansion. After strenuous negotiations, Gilcrease contracted to purchase the collection for $250,000. Although this price was a bargain, averaging $350 per item, still it necessitated installment payments over several years between the signing of the agreement in 1944 and the delivery of the collection in 1947.

The Funeral, 1900–1910.
Joseph Henry Sharp. 18.375 x 30.5,
oil/canvas, GM 0137.313.

The Burial, 1890-1910.
Joseph Henry Sharp. 26.375 x
36.625, oil/canvas, GM 0137.385.

OVERLEAF: *Dividing the Chief's
Estate,* 1890-1910. Joseph Henry
Sharp. 37.5 x 51, oil/canvas,
GM 0137.388.

COLE AND SHARP

By the end of Joseph Henry Sharp's life in 1953, he was best known for his role as founder and active member of the Taos Society of Artists. However, before that he spent more than a decade working on the Crow Reservation in Montana, painting scenes of the Indians' daily lives and completing a remarkable series of Indian portraits, including many survivors of the Battle of the Little Big Horn. Not surprisingly, it was this work that interested Cole. How well Cole knew Sharp is not known (the artist wrote an illustrated letter to Cole on March 17, 1927), but he acquired one of the most outstanding groups of the artist's work. Among the sixteen oils of daily life is a funeral cycle that demonstrates the value of Sharp's long time spent on the reservation. Observed in the winter, the cycle shows *The Funeral* and *The Burial,* and also the aftermath, *Dividing the Chief's Estate.* The fifty-four portraits of American Indian men and women are not only an important and accurate record of real sitters, but also beautifully rendered.

Letter to Philip Cole from Joseph Henry Sharp, dated March 17, 1927. GM 1337.1046.

Gilcrease beside the plane that transported him on trips to New York during his negotiations for the Cole estate.

BIBLIOGRAPHY

Hunt, David. "The Old West Revisited: The Private World of Doctor Philip Cole," *American Scene,* vol. 8, no. 4, 1967.

Joyner, Brooks. "Gilcrease Museum and the American Western Collection of Dr. Philip Gillette Cole." *Gilcrease Journal,* 9 (Summer 2001)

Ladner, Mildred D. *O. C. Seltzer, Painter of the Old West.* Norman, OK: University of Oklahoma Press, 1979.

Milsten, David Randolph. *Thomas Gilcrease.* San Antonio, TX: Naylor Co., 1969.

FACING: *Prowlers of the Prairie,* 1926. Olaf Seltzer. 43.875 x 53.875, oil/canvas, GM 0137.898.

Had one of a couple of near misses hit the mark, Gilcrease would never have acquired the Cole collection. A family recollection indicates that before Cole's death, he had discussed the possibility of leaving the collection to the Montana Historical Society, which was planning to build a state museum. Cole's stipulation that a special wing be built to exhibit the collection may have been the deal breaker. A closer call came during Gilcrease's negotiations when the R. W. Norton Foundation (now the R. W. Norton Museum in Shreveport, Louisiana) offered $400,000. Gilcrease, who had been holding out for a price lower than the final $250,000, saw the value and closed the deal.

Gilcrease contracted to purchase the Cole collection while living in San Antonio. By the time the final installment was paid, he was in Tulsa, where he took delivery of the crated artworks. Perhaps if he had been able to take ownership of the collection earlier and to display it in Texas, the public's response to his San Antonio museum would have been more positive and Gilcrease would not have closed it in 1947. Fortunately for Tulsa, Gilcrease moved his collection there that year and worked over the next two years to ready the Thomas Gilcrease Museum for its opening in 1949—with the artworks from the Cole collection as a highlight. As part of the contract, the sale was kept confidential for two years, which made the collection's exhibition debut even more exciting. Most Americans did not know about the existence of the Cole collection, and the few who did know had been wondering about its disposition since it dropped out of sight after Cole's death.

The Cole collection was Gilcrease's first acquisition of a large group of fine art from a single source. Most importantly, it represented an enormous leap forward in connoisseurship as Gilcrease benefited from the previous owner's thirty years of thoughtful assembly of some of the finest works of western art. During the time Cole was actively seeking the best of the western artists, he had the opportunity to work directly with some of them, such as Charles Russell. Correspondence between Cole and Nancy Russell, who acted as her husband's agent, reveals Cole as a selective, even demanding, collector. Gilcrease could be just as demanding, expecting the best, backed by his ability to pay for it. Thomas Gilcrease no doubt would have liked Philip Gillette Cole had the two ever met. Cole, like Gilcrease, was very private, collecting things he loved in order to be surrounded by them, for posterity and not for investment. Both men had an affinity for western culture and art, had the resources to obtain what they wanted, and developed a great deal of knowledge about what they were collecting. But Gilcrease did not know Cole, or, ironically, even know of him until after Cole's death. But how fitting it is that after Cole spent a lifetime collecting, his collection became part of Gilcrease's, who also spent his lifetime collecting. Cole would surely have appreciated that Gilcrease continued the work Cole had started.

Your Excellency's

Most Obedient &

Very Humb: Serv:
&c.

B Franklin

Silas Deane

Commissioners Plenipotentiary
for the United States of
North America

"No one else knew the location of the books as well, and when he would seek out one of the rare volumes…he had a way of opening a book lightly and with such caution that one would have thought every page would disappear when he touched it."

—DAVID RANDOLPH MILSTEN ON THOMAS GILCREASE

Above, Gilcrease as a younger man.

FACING: Detail of a letter from Benjamin Franklin and Silas Deane to Baron Schulenberg, Prussian Minister of State for Frederick the Great, dated February 14, 1777. GM 4076.3914.

THOMAS GILCREASE was not only a collector of artwork and archaeological artifacts but a notable bibliophile; he had a consuming passion for acquiring books, manuscripts, maps, and other historical materials relating to American Indian culture and early American history. A mover and shaker in the antiquarian book world of the 1940s and 50s, the oilman and collector compiled a comprehensive library collection that exemplified diverse aspects of the American narrative. If an item told a story about America, particularly if it made reference to the settlement of the trans-Mississippi West or to the history and traditions of the American Indian, Mr. Gilcrease attempted to acquire it. Eudotia Teenor, Gilcrease's longtime secretary, once said of him that his "hunger for cultural and historical knowledge…spurred him on in his endeavor to make his collection of Americana the finest." Gilcrease traveled the globe and spent many years of his life in his effort to attain this goal, building a collection that stands today as one the finest of its kind in the world.

A major focus of the Gilcrease library collection is the American Indian. Throughout his career as a collector, Thomas Gilcrease endeavored to gather, maintain, and preserve materials important to understanding the history and traditions of the native peoples of the Americas. Edwin Wolf II, biographer of preeminent bookseller A. S. W. Rosenbach wrote of Gilcrease's efforts to create a collection that would enlighten the world on the subject of America's indigenous peoples, "He also built a magnificent art gallery and library on the grounds and …began filling his museum with rare Indian relics…books about Indians and manuscripts concerning them…Gilcrease possessed a passionate desire to have the white man understand Indian culture. "

When ownership of the museum was transferred to the city of Tulsa, Oklahoma, in 1955, the Thomas Gilcrease Institute of American History and Art was presented to the people with the provision that the museum be "devoted to the free public enjoyment of the artistic, cultural and historical record of the American Indian."

Thirlestaine House, Cheltenham England. Sir Thomas Phillipps removed his household and all his collections from Middle Hill in Worcestershire to Thirlestaine House in Cheltenham during the years 1864-1865.

Sir Thomas Phillipps.
Below, Gilcrease, ca. 1925.

Items Thomas Gilcrease collected for his library included manuscripts, maps and atlases, rare books, photographs, newspapers, and broadsides. Several large collections helped build the foundation of his substantial assemblage of Americana. When Gilcrease acquired the art collection of New York physician Philip G. Cole in the 1940s, he simultaneously acquired a large number of books, photographs, and manuscripts on western American history and American Indian life that Cole had amassed. Around the same time he obtained another significant collection, that of Oklahoma historian Grant Foreman. Foreman and his wife Caroline spent years of their lives writing about the Oklahoma region and the American Indians who lived there. The couple searched for material throughout the United States, examining thousands of documents in the National Archives, the Library of Congress, and the Newberry Library in Chicago, as well as in many other libraries and historical societies across the country. Continuing their research abroad, the Foremans located important information in the British Museum, the Public Records Office in London, and the Bibliotheque Nationale de Paris. The couple took copious notes, sometimes copying sources verbatim, which are now a part of the library at Gilcrease Museum. In addition, they collected many books in the field of their scholarship (in fact the underpinnings of their house had to be reinforced due to the heavy weight of the books); the Americana books of the Foreman library were also acquired by Thomas Gilcrease.

In 1946, Gilcrease acquired the collection of Lester Hargrett, at which time Hargrett was hired as director of the Gilcrease Foundation, a position he held for three years. Hargrett's collection included thousands of rare items, many relating to colonial America, the Five Civilized Tribes, and the American West. Also during this period Mr. Gilcrease acquired a considerable amount of materials from the library of one of the greatest book collectors of all time, Sir Thomas Phillipps of England. After Phillipps's death in 1872, his monumental library was dispersed in a series of sales that continued for decades. The materials purchased by Gilcrease included numerous notes and sketches by the artist George Catlin and the journal of Luke Foxe, written during his voyage in search of a northwestern passage in 1631. Hispanic material also interested Gilcrease. In the early 1950s he acquired the collection of George Robert Graham Conway, an Englishman living in Mexico who had for almost thirty years collected 16th- through 18th-century manuscripts relating to the Spanish colonies in South and Central America.

In addition to purchasing whole collections, Thomas Gilcrease procured select materials from dealers and auctions. An article in the February 7, 1945 *New York Times* reported an acquisition he made from the auction of an Americana collection formed by C. G. Littell of Chicago: "... a copy of the first edition of Archibald Loudon's 'A Selection of Some of the Most Interesting Narratives of the Outrages Committed by the Indians in Their Wars With the White

La pesche des Sauuages p. 15
passinassiopeK Je decris cette pesche ailleur qui est une des
chofes tres merueilleuffes touchand La F. 19 Pesche

Kouabagan

atiꞵanek

BateʃKoupan

eʃkan

Instrumens pour La pesche

THE CODEX CANADIENSIS

Many purchases were made during Gilcrease's travels abroad. In 1949, he acquired the *Codex Canadiensis* from Henry Stevens, Son, & Stiles in London. A bound volume of 180 drawings of the peoples, flora, and fauna native to 17th-century New France, the work is attributed to Jesuit missionary Louis Nicolas and is among the library's most prized possessions.

Codex Canadiensis,
late 17th century. GM 4726.7.

Thomas Gilcrease, Dr. Nelson Glueck and others looking at Hispanic documents. Gilcrease Museum. Inset at right, Cortez Decree, 1521. GM 4075.3916.

THE CORTEZ DECREE

On November 8, 1519, Hernan Cortez led his men into the Aztec capital of Tenochtitlan. Built on an island in Lake Texcoco, the city boasted a population of 30,000, larger than most European cities. Within two years of his historic entry, Cortez had captured the city. This document is one of the earliest known decrees issued by Cortez after the fall of Tenochtitlan in 1521. It instructs his men to search all Aztecs leaving the city for gold and jewels.

People' went to the Thomas Gilcrease Foundation for $430." According to Gilcrease's secretary Eudotia Teenor, he had frequent dealings with "Rosenbach Co., NY, Goodspeed's Book Shop, Boston, Edward Eberstadt & Sons, NY, Kennedy Galleries, NY, Wm. H. Robinson, Ltd., London, Henry Stevens Sons & Stiles, London, and Earl Stendhal, Hollywood." The Rosenbach Company, with offices in New York and Philadelphia, sold Gilcrease some of the most notable documents in his collection. In December 1949 he acquired items that included the Bernaldez Codex, which gives an account of Christopher Columbus's voyages; two manuscripts written by Diego Columbus (one dated 1512 and thought to be the earliest extant letter from the New World); the first decree made by Hernan Cortez the day after he captured the Aztec capital of Tenochtitlan in 1521; and a letter written by Hernandez de Soto to Hernan Ponce de Leon when both men were serving under Pizarro in Peru.

Thomas Gilcrease also sought to preserve documents that provided insight into the founding of the United States. In 1950, he made a second major purchase from the Rosenbachs that included a document certifying Paul Revere to act as messenger for the Massachusetts Committee of Safety; a letter written by Thomas Jefferson dated July 1, 1776; and a letter sent to the Prussian ambassador by Benjamin Franklin and Silas Deane penned in 1777. With this last item were included certified copies of the American Declaration of Independence and the Articles of Confederation. These documents had recently returned from their display on the American Freedom Foundation's "Freedom Train" traveling exhibition after World War II. The Freedom Train completed a 37,160-mile tour that lasted from September 17, 1947 to January 22, 1949. Visiting every state in the union, the exhibit featured over 100 of the nation's most prized historical documents drawn from private collections as well as the Library of Congress and the National Archives.

Below, The Freedom Train. Inset, Letter from Benjamin Franklin and Silas Deane to Baron Schulenberg, Prussian Minister of State for Frederick the Great, dated February 14, 1777. GM 4076.3914.

"Freedom Tr

Clockwise from upper right, Thomas Gilcrease with books from his collection, 1954. Eliot Elisofon/Life Magazine. ©Time, Inc.; Judy Nichols and Margaret Wiesendanger in the Gilcrease Museum Library, San Antonio, ca. 1943. GM 4327.7943; Gilcrease with schoolchildren.

OVERLEAF: American Sive from *Theatrum Orbis Terrarum*. Abraham Ortelius. Antwerp, 1573. GM 3935.62.

Martin Wiesendanger, the first director of the Gilcrease Museum, commented on the overseas market regarding American materials, "The items have come from all over the world and, strangely enough, London is the best market for manuscripts about the southwest Indians; Oklahoma the most expensive." He went on to explain that "the colonial officials had first contact with the Indians and sent their treaties back to England. Hence the excellent London market." Robert Lee Humber, lifelong friend to Thomas Gilcrease, recounted that "Often were the occasions when we discussed books and manuscripts, and visited the book shops in both America and France. The 'bouquinistes' along the Seine in Paris were always a fascinating diversion for us both. He acquired many priceless memorabilia and documents of rare historical value…Mr. Gilcrease loved books, and his library was 'a dukedom large enough' to fill his years."

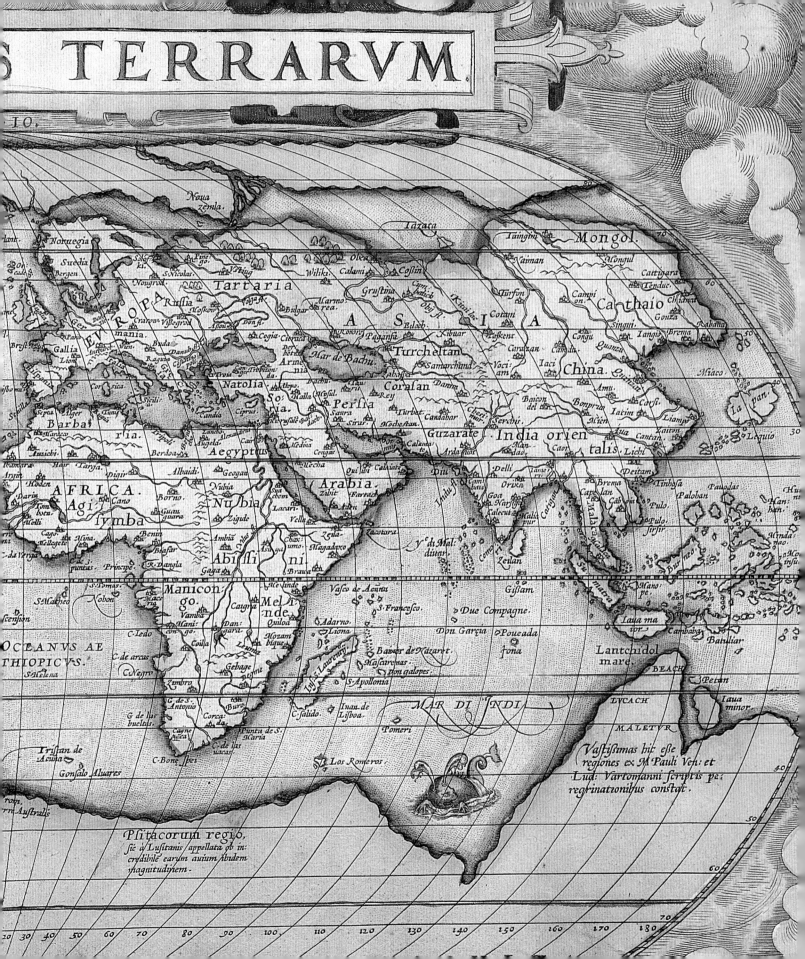

This library that was "a dukedom" arose from a persistent quest but ended as a morass of disordered materials in need of a shepherd. In 1955, Gilcrease Museum director James T. Forrest recommended Martin Wenger of the Colorado Historical Society as first librarian to the collection. He urged Wenger to visit Tulsa, hoping he would accept a position that would place him in charge of the large gathering of material. After Wenger's extensive tour of the library he said, "Jim, this is truly an amazing collection. I had anticipated that it would be primarily made up of manuscripts….to my astonishment this is a library of Americana and its magnitude

Below, Gilcrease seated beneath a portrait of his daughter Des Cygnes by Howard Chandler Christy

FACING: Gilcrease ca. 1935; Don Miguel de Cendoya coat of arms. GM 4076.8514.

is difficult to assess. It offers a terrific challenge to a librarian!" Wenger accepted the appointment and served the library at Gilcrease for eight years. During his tenure, he grew to appreciate Thomas Gilcrease's deep knowledge of the holdings he had gathered. If origins could not be traced through office records, he would consult the collector, who would answer his questions promptly.

Thomas Gilcrease's significant achievements in collecting were aided by his early interest in American materials. The study and collecting of Americana—defined by rare book dealer Charles P. Everitt as "anything showing how and why people came here, and how they lived after they got here"— was a new and previously ignored field. Attempting to piece together the story of the Americas' earlier inhabitants as well as preserving something of the struggles, adventures, ideals, and aspirations of those who settled the New World, Thomas Gilcrease may have accomplished even more than he intended. The holdings of Gilcrease Museum reflect a devotion to safeguard the history of America and to share it with its people.

Building a Museum:
The Gilcrease Institute

Building a Museum: The Gilcrease Institute

GARY MOORE, ASSISTANT DIRECTOR, GILCREASE MUSEUM

Gilcrease in Athens, Greece, 1926. GM 4327.7824.

FACING: Thomas Gilcrease, 1950. Background, aerial view of Gilcrease grounds.

IT GENERALLY COMES AS A SURPRISE to those unfamiliar with the personal history of Thomas Gilcrease that more than one "Gilcrease Museum" has existed. But, in fact, one could argue that there have actually been three such institutions. Understanding what drove Mr. Gilcrease to create these museums and how they migrated and changed over the years requires delving into the personality of this man who was so driven to "leave a track."

In reviewing both David Milsten's biography of Thomas Gilcrease and other pertinent sources, it is difficult to discern when Mr. Gilcrease first had the germ of an idea to both collect art and become a museum builder. Perhaps it was during his visit to the San Francisco World's Fair in 1915, seven years after his marriage to his young Osage bride, Belle. He did purchase two bronze sculptures there, although they were of no lasting significance. Or it could have been the product of his many world travels afforded by his newfound wealth and the personal contacts he established, such as his enduring friendship with Robert Lee Humber, a museum builder himself, having been the primary catalyst behind the creation of the North Carolina Museum of Art.

I believe, though admittedly this is based on anecdotal material, that Gilcrease was motivated by two forces. First, he was a voracious learner, as evidenced by many things, including the fact that he taught himself more than one foreign language. Second, he was an astute emulator. Since he began his art collecting and museum building as one unfamiliar with the field, he accomplished much of what he did by assessing the achievements of others. What he did not know about museums, he learned from intimate friends such as Dr. Humber and also the plethora of other museum builders of his age, such as Henry Huntington and Andrew Mellon.

But beyond this emulation was a restlessness of spirit to do something of permanent value. It became the driving force of his life, lasting well beyond either of his two ill-fated marriages or, for that matter, any human relationship. Perhaps because his wealth had essentially been, to his way of thinking, a gift or mere luck of the draw, he had no great abiding interest in his oil business. It merely became the means to an end. And that end was to leave something behind that would endure far beyond his years.

Although Thomas Gilcrease accumulated his wealth primarily through drilling activities in the historic Glenn Pool oil field and incorporated Gilcrease Oil Company under the laws of the state of Oklahoma in 1922, economic conditions eventually compelled him to dissolve that corporation and establish Gilcrease Oil Company of Texas, headquartered in San Antonio. There he bought an historic structure known as the Casino Club in 1942, renamed it the Gilcrease Building, and converted its sixth floor into a museum capable of housing his budding art collection.

Prior to transferring the collection to San Antonio, Gilcrease stored his valuable works in Tulsa under conditions that might be considered less than pristine by today's museum accreditation standards. He had employed Cephas Stout, a part-Cherokee whom he affectionately referred to as "Chief," to perform many maintenance and renovation tasks around his stone house and gardens. During this period of transition, he instructed Stout to convert his garage and barn to storehouses for the art and artifacts. Gilcrease jokingly referred to the barn as his gallery and the garage as his library.

The Casino Club was located at the intersection of Presa and Crockett streets and was a six-floor Art Deco structure originally constructed in 1927 to house the activities of an exclusive social organization known as the San Antonio Casino Club. The edifice, with its distinctive tiered dome, was an interesting choice to house an art museum as it was designed to contain kitchen facilities, club rooms, dining rooms, and a ballroom to accommodate the dances and other activities of the social elite.

It is no surprise, then, that the pictures of the first Gilcrease Museum depict a rather posh setting for the oilman's art collection, and it was, in fact, the ballroom that became the museum's main gallery while the banquet hall was converted to a space to house library holdings. The museum opened in 1943 under the name "Thomas Gilcrease Collection by the Thomas Gilcrease Foundation," and its first director was Martin Wiesendanger, who had been so instrumental in the formation of the collection itself. Many might have been content to live with the tepid public response that the Gilcrease collection received in San Antonio, but Mr. Gilcrease demonstrated that he was not willing to see what had become the all-consuming component of his existence simply a footnote to that city's history. So, in 1947, he closed the museum in Texas and moved his holdings back to Tulsa, yet another example of the restlessness that drove him to get his collection before as many people as possible. Still, he chose Tulsa as his next venue even though other cities might have provided a more rapid leap to the national stage. Tulsa was home, and that home had, after all, provided the basis for his wealth.

Construction of the Gilcrease Museum entrance. Above, Gilcrease Museum as it appeared shortly after opening in May 1949.

Gilcrease had continued to build the collection, even in the midst of his unsuccessful venture in San Antonio, and he was acutely aware that the modest buildings that had been modified to store his now burgeoning collection would not be adequate to display his works. He engaged the volunteer assistance of his friend Alexander Hogue, who was both an amazingly forward thinking eco-conscious artist and professor of art at the University of Tulsa. One of Hogue's challenges was to create a design that would successfully display Gilcrease's collections yet protect the view of Tulsa's scenic Signal Hill from the museum owner's modest stone residence, a structure which still stands on museum property.

The result of Hogue's efforts was the creation of Quonset hut beams formed in the shape of a U, which thus tied the existing carriage buildings together, pulling the collections under one roof on the Tulsa property for the first time. Mr. Gilcrease appreciated the design because it reminded him of an Indian "long house," a structure used by more than one Native American tribe, which was generally a rectangular structure with a barrel roof. That concept was retained when the museum saw major expansion completed in 1987, and one can still easily observe the barrel roof extending from the entry of the museum throughout the main corridor.

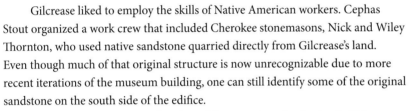

Certificate of Civic Recognition, 1949. Gilcrease Museum.

Members of Gilcrease Foundation and construction workers. Back row, from left to right: Cephas Stout, Woody Crumbo, Ed Gilcrease, Lester Hargrett, Katherine Whitehorn, G. B. Bancroft, Pierce Larkin, C.H. Lamb, Thomas Gilcrease, Frank Walling, Legus Chalakee, Nick Thornton, Charlie Breiteau. Seated, left to right: unidentified man, unidentified man, Ezra Stout, unidentified man, Josiah Davis, unidentified man, Jim Stout, Wylie Thornton, unidentified man, Dave Bible. GM 4327.8069b. Construction on Gilcrease Museum, 1963.

Gilcrease liked to employ the skills of Native American workers. Cephas Stout organized a work crew that included Cherokee stonemasons, Nick and Wiley Thornton, who used native sandstone quarried directly from Gilcrease's land. Even though much of that original structure is now unrecognizable due to more recent iterations of the museum building, one can still identify some of the original sandstone on the south side of the edifice.

Gilcrease Museum opened to the public as a private institution in Tulsa on May 3, 1949, and all seemed well for the oil millionaire—his private collection now occupied a fitting home and its reputation was beginning to grow significantly. By this time, Mr. Gilcrease's marriage to Norma Smallwood was well behind him, and by all accounts he had long since lost the desire to expand his oil business. He was content to continue to build his collection, travel, and share relationships with contemporaries from Native American artists such as Acee Blue Eagle to historians such as J. Frank Dobie to fellow museum builders such as Robert Lee Humber.

This period of contentedness, regrettably, did not endure. By 1954, financial reality had finally caught up with Mr. Gilcrease's purchasing binge. The Korean War had caused him to miscalculate investments, and oil pumping activity was limited by government proration. Gilcrease found himself faced with the very real possibility of having to sell components of the collection to satisfy a staggering $2.25 million debt. But selling any portion of what had become his mission in life was anathema to him even though his holdings in full had been appraised at over $12 million dollars. He preferred to keep the collection intact. Not surprisingly, there were many interested parties, including a very strong bid from the city of Claremore, Oklahoma, already home to the Will Rogers Memorial, which sought to add the Gilcrease collection to its assets.

Clockwise from top left, Gilcrease and Gilcrease Foundation members. GM 4327.8067; Gilcrease in front of a portrait of Quanah Parker; standing beside the first painting he purchased, *Rural Courtship.*

OVERLEAF: Gilcrease and Robert Humber, 1949.

THE THOMAS GILCREASE INSTITUTE OF
AMERICAN HISTORY AND ART
OWNED AND OPERATED BY THE CITY OF TULSA

NOTICE

rcrease Institute is undergoing
ensive construction. The
rior is being remodeled. Your
ration in exercising caution while
e museum will be appreciated.

Mr. Ed K. Ellis, Chairman
Bldg. Program - Bd. of Directors

At right, Gilcrease in 1950.
Inset at left, postcards showing
the galleries at Gilcrease, 1959.
Background image, construction
in 1963.

And the line of suitors was hardly limited to the immediate area. Both the University of Oklahoma and the University of Texas approached Gilcrease, expanding on the Red River rivalry of the gridiron. Gilcrease's friend and mentor Robert Lee Humber of North Carolina expressed very strong interest in acquiring the collection for the North Carolina Museum of Art, and Gilcrease seemed on the verge of making that commitment. Then, in the midst of many hastily conceived plans— Gilcrease's creditors were unrelenting in their pressure—a group of Tulsa citizens set in motion an alternative that would eventually secure the oilman's collection for Tulsa.

It began as a private fundraising effort with fits and starts that produced little results in terms of significant cash. Alfred Aaronson, a fellow oilman and a civic-minded leader who was the catalyst behind the growth of Tulsa's public library system, approached Tom Gilcrease with a plea to delay his move to North Carolina so that the voters of Tulsa could be given the opportunity to spend their own money to save Gilcrease Museum for Tulsa.

A bond issue proposal was hastily concocted and presented to Tulsa's mayor, L. C. Clark, who while not opposed to the initiative outright was concerned that the addition of a vote on a bond issue to keep the Gilcrease collections in Tulsa would decrease support for the municipal auditorium already in front of the public. He thus charged the Gilcrease committee with raising the money for the cost of the special election, and the same private citizens who had already given personally to the effort again proved worthy to the task and raised the necessary funds for the bond vote.

Despite a meager turnout, on August 24, 1954 voters approved the initiative to pay the personal debts of Thomas Gilcrease by a three-to-one margin. The municipal auditorium initiative was defeated, confirming Mayor Clark's fears. In exchange for the bond issue proceeds being utilized for payment to his creditors, Thomas Gilcrease signed his collection over to the city of Tulsa through a trust indenture document that endures today as the overriding document for the management and care of the Gilcrease collection.

Thomas Gilcrease devoted future oil royalties to the repayment of his debt to Tulsa, a feat which was not fully accomplished until 1987. It was a significant moment: the settling of that debt meant that he had truly given, not sold, his collection to the citizens of Tulsa. The oilman, collector, and philanthropist continued to live in the modest stone house on museum property until his death in 1962. His final years were filled with travel and art purchases through his foundation, but, perhaps more importantly, with the satisfaction of knowing his collection remained intact and his legacy secure.

Patron, Friend, and Collector

CAROLE KLEIN, ASSOCIATE CURATOR OF ART, GILCREASE MUSEUM

MOST CULTURES VALUE AND RESPECT THE ARTS, as evidenced by the long history of patronage in its many forms—patronage by individuals, communities, governments, and corporations. Some patrons seek prestige, others buy for investment, and many simply want the pleasure of looking at beautiful objects. Whatever the motives, some of the world's greatest works of art might never have been created without some type of patronage. It is integral to the development of the arts. Material and emotional sustenance for artists promotes conditions under which they can produce their best work. Patrons with ideas of their own can be stimulating to an artist's creativity—or can sometimes be detrimental. Yet even conflicts between artist and patron can reshape and crystallize an artist's philosophy, leading to art that otherwise might never have been conceived. The ramifications of the interaction between artists and patrons are as endless as the personalities involved.

Beginning in the early 1940s, Thomas Gilcrease sought art from individual artists in order to build his collection. Developing friendships with many, he had an eye for their finest work, purchasing in many instances the best an artist produced. Gilcrease commissioned works as well, encouraging creativity and expecting quality. A nurturing patron, he was generous, sometimes paying more than the artist asked and always on time with payments.

Gilcrease extended patronage beyond monetary arrangements. He was an encouraging yet forthright critic. He challenged artists, engaging them to explore their ideas and sometimes his. He asked them to record their thoughts and what they hoped to portray, feeling this would add to the value and interest of their work for generations to come. He provided opportunities for them to exhibit, sometimes in a group, sometimes in one-man shows, giving them the exposure needed to become

Superstition, detail, ca. 1921.
Ernest L. Blumenschein. 50.25
x 49, oil/canvas, GM 0137.531.

successful. Overall, he inspired and championed the artists he admired, and mutual respect prevailed in his relationships with them. His nurturing of artists, often at a time when they could appreciate it most, helped shape their careers. The artists' perceptions of Gilcrease, revealed in their words, help flesh out the aura of the collector.

Three artists became close associates of Gilcrease and entered into salaried contracts with him that lasted for several years. Under Gilcrease's patronage they produced some of their finest works, which then became part of his collection. These artists are Acee Blue Eagle (Creek/Pawnee), Woodrow "Woody" Crumbo (Potawatomi), and sculptor Willard Stone, who was part Cherokee. They are among the most important Native American artists of the 20th century.

Thomas Gilcrease, Acee Blue Eagle, and Willard Stone.

Acee Blue Eagle. GM 4327.7611.

Buffalo Hunt. Acee Blue Eagle.
18.875 x 34.875, tempera/paper,
GM 0227.408.

ACEE BLUE EAGLE (1907-1959)

"a grand person to me outside of our business. . . "

Acee Blue Eagle (Alex C. McIntosh), an artist who achieved worldwide acclaim, was also a lecturer and art educator and the grandson of William McIntosh, a Creek chief. Gilcrease acquired approximately fifty paintings from the artist. The encouragement and material assistance he received from Gilcrease helped sustain Blue Eagle during some of his most productive years. He was encouraged by Gilcrease to paint works relating to his Creek heritage. His *Creek Chiefs* is an homage to the many Creek chiefs who were members of the McIntosh clan.

There was a special bond between Gilcrease and Blue Eagle based in part on their common Creek heritage. A letter from the artist to Gilcrease begins "How is my ol' Creek Injun frien' "? Another says "Greetings my friend and tribesman!" Gilcrease in a letter to Blue Eagle in 1951 writes, "The first time you are up this way, please give me the pleasure of seeing you smile and evidence of a Creek Indian's happy spirit. Don't wait too long. We will have plenty of jerky for you."

Blue Eagle announced his pending marriage and asked for an advance of $400 on his account: "I need some money for the wedding…I have to buy the rings, marriage expenses and a short honeymoon! I am looking forward to you meeting her—I know you will love her for the grand person she is—she thinks you are grand even though she hasn't met you yet!"

Blue Eagle identified an aspect of Gilcrease's character that formed the foundation of the collector's relationship with creative individuals: "You have been indeed a grand person to me outside of our business, and beyond that connection you have touched my heart with your personal feelings and soul…you have a spiritual quality about you that is carried over to people of a creative talent!"

Warriors on Horses. Acee Blue Eagle.
19 x 29.25, tempera/paper, GM 0227.458.

FACING: *Creek Chiefs.* Acee Blue Eagle.
15.5 x 16, tempera/paper, GM 0227.469.

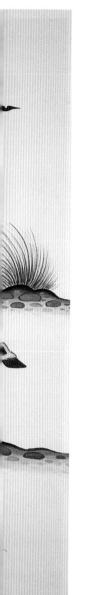

WOODROW WILSON CRUMBO (1912-1989)

"as if to say beauty is love. . . "

Thomas Gilcrease met Woody Crumbo in 1945 at the Mayo Hotel in Tulsa. He purchased twenty-seven paintings from the artist in 1946 and employed him to help find and select art and artifacts for the collection. Crumbo would come to have a successful and diversified career as artist, poet, Indian dancer, art director of Bacone College, a museum curator and director. He had an astute eye for Indian and non-Indian art of the West and was ready to travel with Gilcrease on a moment's notice to visit galleries and artists. When in his twenties, he had been a part-time resident of the Taos art colony. Accompanying Gilcrease to Taos in 1945, he introduced him to Joseph Henry Sharp and other artists. This timely meeting presented Gilcrease with a stellar opportunity to acquire what are now considered some of the masterworks of the Taos Society of Artists.

Crumbo considered his time with Gilcrease valuable—an education in itself. "I acquired a liberal education in the type of arts I am interested in while I was with you, and couldn't have gotten more any other place in America. My association with you is worth more to me than a four year college course."

Gilcrease remodeled a house on his property, installing a large north window, and established Crumbo there as an artist-in-residence. The artist produced over 150 works for Gilcrease, among them masterpieces such as *Burial Ceremony—Spirits Ascending* and *Peyote Religious Ceremony.* One of Crumbo's peyote, or messenger, birds became a symbol for the museum and was at one time painted on the exterior of the building over the entrance. The artist achieved wide acclaim for his paintings. He is also known for his determined efforts to promote other artists and students such as Willard Stone. His perceptive observations about Gilcrease speak of the collector's love of life: "I learned to appreciate and admire his keen sense of respect and love for all things about him, whether it was a work of art, a human being, or things of nature. By the same token he would use his great enthusiasm and personality to inspire another to go along with his plans; he would plant flowers, trees, and shrubs around and about the museum as it was being built and they would respond to his kind and gentle touch with flower bloom or fruit as if to say beauty is love."

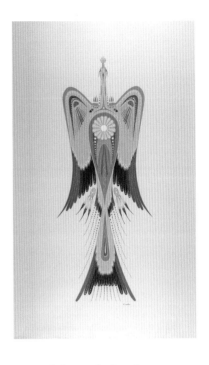

Inset at left, Woody Crumbo.

Peyote Bird. Woody Crumbo.
18.5 x 35.5, watercolor/paper,
GM 0227.505.

Burial Ceremony—Spirit Ascending.
Woody Crumbo. 14.5 x 28, tempera
and watercolor/paper, GM 0227.483.

OVERLEAF, *Peyote Religious
Ceremony.* Woody Crumbo.
11.25 x 19.5, tempera/paper,
GM 0227.577.

WILLARD STONE (1916-1985)

"If my work . . . did not tell a story, he knew I had a dull knife."

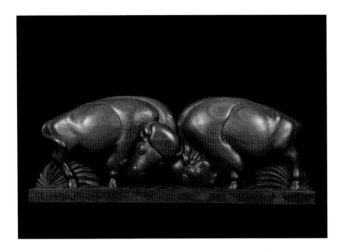

Thomas Gilcrease employed woodcarver Willard Stone, student of Woody Crumbo and Acee Blue Eagle, under a three-year contract beginning in 1946. This period gave Stone financial security and allowed him to grow as an artist, both conceptually and technically. Gilcrease encouraged him to explore contemporary ideas and to discuss his work and philosophy. Stone, referring to a conversation between himself, Gilcrease, and Acee Blue Eagle, says in a letter to Gilcrease in 1946, "I got some different ideas about religion from the conversation that night." Stone produced over fifty carvings for Gilcrease. Among them are some of his most important works including *Lady of Spring, Unity of Purpose,* and *Tomorrow.* His works depicting nuclear weapons, world politics, and the influence of Christianity on Native Americans demonstrate Stone's philosophical bent and social awareness. He became nationally recognized as a premier woodcarver who had a way of telling a story that remains unique.

Stone gives insight into Gilcrease the art critic: "Mr. Gilcrease could judge works of art, not only as to subject matter, but he understood composition and perspective. If my work or finished carving did not tell a story, he knew I had a dull knife and found a way to let me know without hurting my pride. He was as much an artist as the artist." Gilcrease eventually acquired some 500 paintings by over 100 Native American artists, helping to support them as he collected works that presented the Native American story. His support of regional artists had a direct bearing on their role in the history of Native American art.

Explaining the effect of Gilcrease's patronage upon his career, Stone realized the opportunity he had experienced: "Tom Gilcrease gave me the chance to find out what I could do with wood and clay and to develop a style of my own. I would not have been recognized had it not been for him, because he gave me the courage to try."

Buffalo Bulls. Willard Stone. 8.875 x 23.75 x 4, wood, GM 1127.23. Stone, holding *The Doctor,* with *Buffalo Bulls* in the backgrond.

FACING: *Lady of Spring* (detail). Willard Stone. 27.75 x 4.75 x 4.5, walnut, GM 1127.76.

JOSEPH HENRY SHARP (1859-1953)

"You have made it possible for me to carry on and do much of my best work the last several years."

Gilcrease became a patron of noted early founders of the Taos Society of Artists, particularly Joseph Henry Sharp, Oscar Berninghaus, Ernest Blumenschein, and Bert Phillips. He felt their work captured the spirit of the unspoiled West. His association with Sharp resulted in friendship and a profitable business relationship. His admiration for Sharp's work over the years is evidenced by the several hundred paintings he purchased from the artist and by the correspondence between the two from the mid 1940s until Sharp's death in 1953. He writes to Sharp in September, 1948: "Had it not been for your great talent, strength and tireless years of painting, the world would have much less beauty and historical past preserved on canvas…I shall always be grateful to you for having done so many fine paintings of the Indians and the early west and for having made it possible for me to preserve these great paintings for the pleasure of all those who pass this way."

Sharp responds to Gilcrease: "… truly the finest letter of appreciation I have ever received… and will be cherished as long as we remain on this glorious earth. Then I hope and expect in spirit to meet you and all those fine Indians we both love so well. You have made it possible for me to carry on and do much of my best work the last several years."

In 1947 Sharp gave his self portrait to Gilcrease and wrote how he painted out the holes and repairs in the hat. He adds, "When in hat store & you can locate a soft Barsolino, or other #7, pick it up and I will wear it all the rest of my life!" Gilcrease sent Sharp a new hat, and Sharp responded, "Hat! You timed well…I can't give up the old one yet—fine to work in any light—afraid it would jinx my technique." Sharp's old hat is in the Gilcrease collection.

Gilcrease requested self-portraits from Berninghaus and Blumenschein and they responded. Bert G. Phillips, feeling that he was not a portraitist, sent a painting of himself by John Young-Hunter. Through the friendship and patronage of Gilcrease, the Taos artists were encouraged to paint until the end of their lives.

Taos artists. Back row from left to right: E. Martin Hennings, Bert Phillips, Victor Higgins, Ernest Blumenschein, J.H. Sharp. Front row from left to right: Walter Ufer, E. Irving Couse, Oscar Berninghaus, Herbert Bush Dunton, and Kenneth Adams. GM 4337.5574. Inset, at far left, Sharp and Gilcrease outside Sharp's studio in Taos, New Mexico, 1949. GM 4337.3087b.

Crucita. Joseph Henry Sharp. 47.5 x 55.5, oil/canvas, GM 0137.2194.

Self Portrait, 1947.
Joseph Henry
Sharp. 24.625 x
20.625, oil/canvas,
GM 0137.323.

Singers of the Night.
Joseph Henry Sharp. 35 x 45.25,
oil/canvas, GM 0137.305.

OSCAR E. BERNINGHAUS (1874-1952)

"Thank you for your nice letter and for the check enclosed"

Gilcrease bought twelve paintings from Berninghaus between the years 1945-1949. Like other artists, he expressed appreciation not only for Gilcrease's purchases, but for his engaging written words: "Thank you for your nice letter and for the check enclosed with it. You always write such interesting and encouraging letters… I appreciate them very much."

Gilcrease was generous and prompt when paying artists. Berninghaus expressed surprise in 1946 at receiving full payment early for a group of paintings and wrote, "Thank you for your check covering the purchase of my paintings. While our understanding was that payments would be more or less divided in the coming months, your payment in full at this time was very pleasant to have."

Self Portrait, 1951. Oscar E. Berninghaus. 19.5 x 15.5, oil/canvas, GM 0137.516.

Left, *Along the Racetrack,* 1948-1949. Oscar E. Berninghaus. 15.25 x 19.25, oil/masonite, GM 0137.514. Below left, *Too Old for the Rabbit Hunt,* 1927. Oscar E. Berninghaus. 34.5 x 39.625, oil/canvas, GM 0137.524.

FACING: *Threshing Time, Taos Pueblo,* 1944. Oscar E. Berninghaus. 25.625 x 30.625, oil/canvas, GM 0137.2086.

OVERLEAF: *After the Dance at the Pueblo, Taos,* 1946. Oscar E. Berninghaus. 25.25 x 29.5, oil/canvas, GM 0137.517.

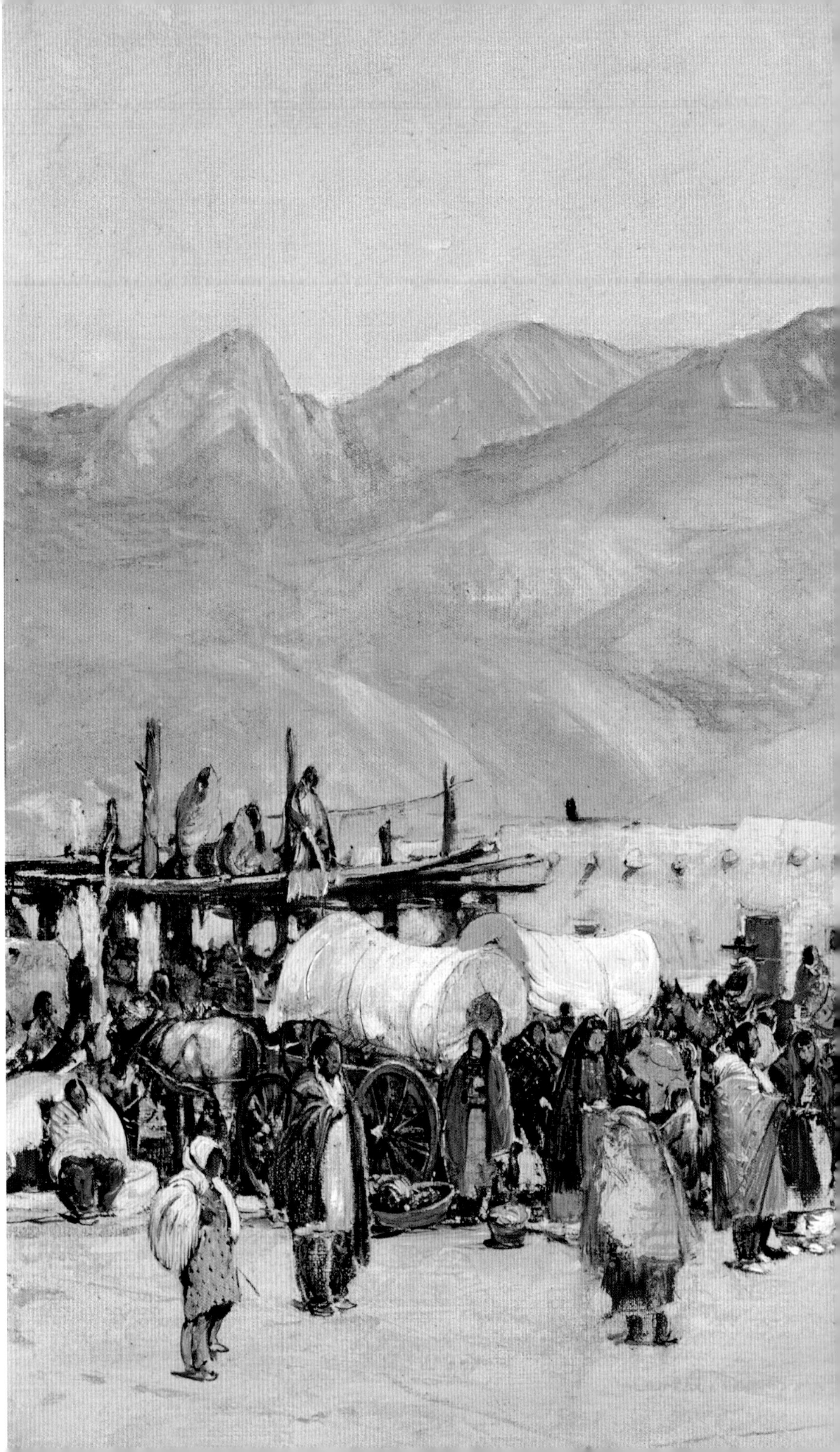

ERNEST L. BLUMENSCHEIN (1874-1960)

"I too felt we had a great deal in common. . ."

Gilcrease purchased only five of Blumenschein's paintings between the years 1945 and 1951, but they are among the artist's finest, including *Superstition, Enchanted Forest,* and *Moon, Morning Star and Evening Star.* He writes to Blumenschein in 1945: "I appreciated greatly my visits to your studio. I had. . . known of you and your work for a number of years and had always wished to meet you. . . . I found all of you older artists of Taos to be really great men in your line of work and fine men to know personally. I am most happy to have each of you well represented in our gallery." Blumenschein responds: "Thanks for your very cordial and friendly letter. . . . I too felt that we had a great deal in common and enjoyed our meeting and conversation."

Self Portrait. Ernest L. Blumenschein. 18.125 x 15.125, gouache and ink/paper, GM 0237.784.

Moon, Morning Star and Evening Star, 1922. Ernest L. Blumenschein. 56.125 x 40, oil/canvas, GM 0137.2192.

FACING: *Enchanted Forest,* 1946. Ernest L. Blumenschein. 56.125 x 40, oil/canvas, GM 0137.2191.

OVERLEAF: *Ranchos Church with Indians.* Ernest L. Blumenschein. 13.375 x 22, oil/panel, GM 0137.2195.

BERT G. PHILLIPS (1868-1956)

Gilcrease bought Phillips's *Taos Deer Hunter* in 1945 from the Blue Door Gallery in Taos. The next year he bought twelve paintings from Phillips which constituted quite a sale for the seventy-seven-year-old artist.

Bert Phillips, 1941. John Young-Hunter. 19.625 x 15.75, oil/canvas, GM 0137.563.

Turkey Hunter, 1946. Bert G. Phillips. 39.625 x 25.75, oil/canvas, GM 0137.523.

FACING: *A Taos Garden.* Bert G. Phillips. 33.25 x 28.625, oil/wood panel, GM 0137.529.

OVERLEAF: *Burial Procession—Penitente Ceremonial—Near Taos.* Bert G. Phillips. 38.5 x 44.625, oil/canvas, GM 0137.2083.

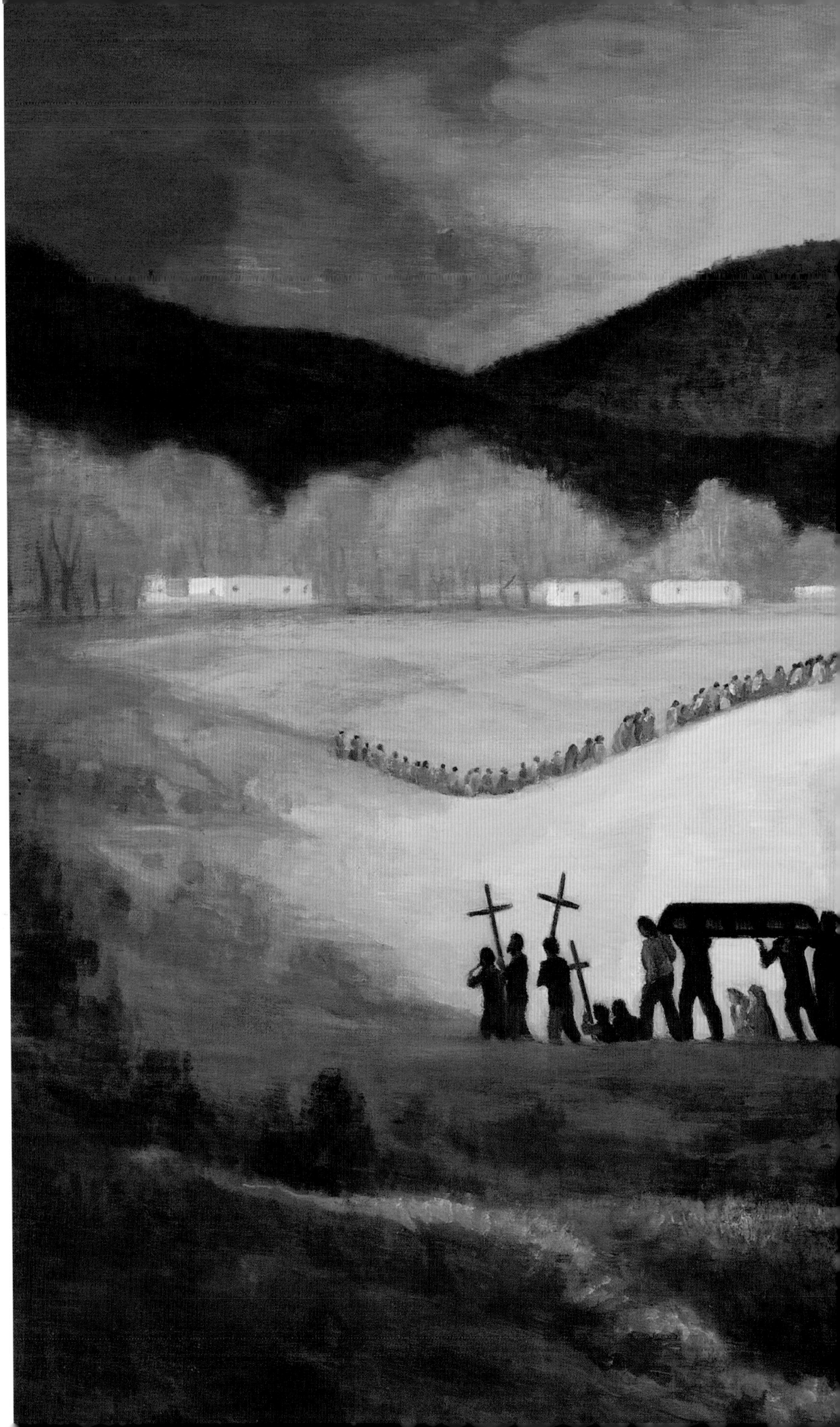

Corn Maidens. Bert G. Phillips.
44.5 x 46.125, oil/canvas,
GM 0137.2197.

Taos Deer Hunter. Bert G. Phillips.
31 x 31, oil/canvas,
GM 0137.2084.

CHARLES BANKS WILSON (BORN 1918)

"Gilcrease was looking for paintings of

American Indians for his museum. . ."

Nationally known illustrator, printmaker, muralist, and portraitist Charles Banks Wilson became known as an Oklahoma treasure. He painted works of historical importance as he portrayed Oklahoma life, history, and its most famous people. In 1944 the Gilcrease Foundation purchased some lithographs from Wilson and sent along a letter explaining that Thomas Gilcrease was looking for paintings of American Indians for his museum and was interested in purchasing Wilson's painting depicting Indian drummers under a hanging light bulb. The painting *Oklahoma Melody* soon became part of the Gilcrease collection, as did *Montana Grandson, Powwow Afternoon,* and *Shawnee Ribbon Bets.* Among the large collection of Wilson's works in Gilcrease Museum is a portrait of James C. Webber, Delaware Chief, probably the only one in existence, which Wilson gave to Gilcrease in 1950.

Wilson and Gilcrease developed a long association. The Institute commissioned Wilson to paint a formal portrait of Thomas Gilcrease. Unveiled in 1959, his portrait puts the figure of Gilcrease at the center of the rolling Osage hills, the original museum building behind him and museum objects at his hand. The image is very much a symbol and a tribute to the man whose collections are enjoyed by people from all over the world.

Charles Banks Wilson, right, with Robert Lindneux, in the Gilcrease galleries. Artist Robert Lindneux was a close friend of Charles M. Russell, and Gilcrease delighted in hearing the many stories of Lindneux's experiences with Russell. Gilcrease provided for an exhibition of Lindneux's work in 1956. After Gilcrease died, Lindneux remembered him fondly, saying, "He was a very intelligent, studious, and noble gentleman; we have had many, many enlightening conversations together."

Oklahoma Melody, 1943. Charles Banks Wilson. 14 x 11, oil/canvas, GM 0127.1466.

Shawnee Ribbon Bets, 1948.
Charles Banks Wilson. 27.25 x 35,
oil/canvas, GM 0127.1468.

A MANY-SIDED MAN

As Wilson gathered the opinions of others about Thomas Gilcrease before painting him, he recalled: "As with any personality such as Thomas Gilcrease, he was a many-sided man. One of his business associates suggested that he be painted as the neat, fastidious gentleman he was. I was anxious to get the opinions of others and talked with one of his gardeners. This man was Indian and knew Tom intimately. He said, 'Don't paint him all dressed up, fix him up in work clothing, comfortable shoes, and paint him like the regular fellow he is.' In retrospect I think both were right."

Charles Banks Wilson with his portrait of Thomas Gilcrease, 1959. GM 4327.5958.

Thomas Gilcrease, 1958. Charles Banks Wilson. 40 x 32, egg tempera/canvas, GM 0127.2300.

ALEXANDER HOGUE (1898–1994)

Alexander Hogue. Charles Banks Wilson. 13.75 x 10.75, charcoal/paper, GM 1327.2229.

Gilcrease Museum, 1946. Alexander Hogue. 13 x 17, graphite/paper, GM 1327.366.

OVERLEAF, *Crucified Land*, 1939. Alexander Hogue. 47.375 x 65.5, oil/canvas, GM 0127.2000.

In 1959 the paintings of Alexander Hogue, painter, printmaker, muralist, and illustrator, were featured at the museum. Recognized for his landscapes related to soil erosion, Hogue became internationally renowned. He led the art department at the University of Tulsa from 1945 to 1968. Gilcrease's friendship with Hogue provided opportunities for the two men to discuss art, particularly traditional art versus the more modern influences, which Gilcrease called "this crazy art." Gilcrease purchased Hogue's *Crucified Land* around 1940. He later engaged Hogue's ideas for the museum building for which the artist made drawings.

VINSON LACKEY (1889-1959)

"painstaking attention to detail"

Vinson Lackey was an Oklahoma writer, historian, and artist. From 1935 to 1945 he was state supervisor and field editor for the Federal Writer's Project and state supervisor of the Oklahoma Historical Records Survey. Having traveled all over the state himself in his search for art, Thomas Gilcrease knew the importance of documenting history that would otherwise fade from public awareness. In 1945 he commissioned Vinson Lackey to research and record the early institutions of Indian Territory. The project took the artist four years to complete. Gilcrease paid him by the piece. Lackey traveled and made sketches of the terrain, utilizing original building plans, elevations, early maps, and other sources, and interviewing early settlers and Indians who lived near the structures or had attended the schools. With painstaking attention to detail, Lackey created 105 paintings, representing a valuable and irreplaceable record of these institutions, most of which are no longer in existence. The Lackey collection was a favorite of Gilcrease's, as he had enjoyed collaborating with the artist on the project.

Vinson Lackey. GM 4327.5957. Inset, *Osage Boarding School.* Vinson Lackey. 9 x 12, oil/canvas, GM 0127.1396. Below, *Hunters' Home, Park Hill.* Vinson Lackey. 9 x 12, oil/canvas, GM 0127.1402.

Howard Chandler Christy, American illustrator, landscape and portrait painter, met Gilcrease through Robert Lee Humber. Gilcrease acquired the portraits, *Chief Bacon Rind,* Osage tribal leader, and *Will Rogers,* in 1949. He commissioned Christy to paint portraits of himself and his daughter, Des Cygne. He also acquired *The Signing of the Constitution,* painted in 1937, the year marking the 150th anniversary of the adoption of the Constitution. The work accompanied the Freedom Train during the national tour of American cities from 1947 to 1949. Gilcrease commissioned more historical scenes, but Christy died before they were executed.

Signing of the Constitution.
Howard Chandler Christy.
oil/canvas, 85 x 80.
GM 0127.2082.

Rufino Tamayo. GM 4347.5946.

SOURCES

Milsten, David Randolph. *Thomas Gilcrease.* San Antonio. Naylor Company, 1969.

Letters, Interviews, Documents, Gilcrease Museum archives.

In addition to those artists he supported, there were others with whom Gilcrease became friends. Thomas L. Lewis, artist and Taos gallery owner, met Gilcrease through Woody Crumbo. He joined Gilcrease at his Wyoming retreat on the Hoback River in Jackson Hole. Gilcrease asked Lewis to paint some western landscapes for him. He used an image of one of these on his 1955 Christmas card. "I just mailed out over 1000 Christmas cards portraying your painting "Spirit of the Canyon". This, no doubt, will cause a lot of interest in your painting … Hoping to visit with you and enjoy some of Mrs. Lewis's coffee—good enough for a Frenchman."

Gilcrease always went out of his way to meet and know artists whose work he collected even if he purchased only a single item and no other association transpired. He is known to have met Paul Manship in 1957 and purchased *Indian Hunter with Dog.* Gilcrease had seen Manship's *Promethius Fountain* at Rockefeller Plaza in New York, and impressed, was determined to meet the artist. He sought out Texas artist Frank Reaugh, instructor to Alexander Hogue. In addition, he met some of the Mexican

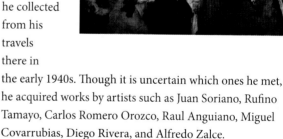

artists whose work he collected from his travels there in the early 1940s. Though it is uncertain which ones he met, he acquired works by artists such as Juan Soriano, Rufino Tamayo, Carlos Romero Orozco, Raul Anguiano, Miguel Covarrubias, Diego Rivera, and Alfredo Zalce.

It is clear that Thomas Gilcrease went beyond the traditional meaning of patronage. The mutual benefits of the coming together of this patron and these artists cannot be measured. His support of artists, not only financially, but emotionally and spiritually, had a far-reaching effect that would grace their lifetimes and reward future generations.

Collecting Antiquity:
Masterpieces from the Ancient Past

ERIC SINGLETON, ASSISTANT CURATOR, GILCREASE MUSEUM

THE COLLECTION OF ANTHROPOLOGICAL artifacts at the Thomas Gilcrease Institute of American History and Art is one of the finest in the world. Containing nearly 320,000 objects, it has been repeatedly praised by private collectors, visiting dignitaries, and academics from all over the world as offering profound support to an understanding of both indigenous and United States history. The depth of the collection makes Gilcrease truly "a museum of the Americas." Cultures represented within it range from the mountains of Alaska to the plains of North America to the deserts of Peru. These cultures have beautiful and rich histories, and it was Thomas Gilcrease's dream to see that they were preserved.

Gilcrease began acquiring items for the collection beginning in the late 1930s. He continued collecting both personally and through his foundation until his death in 1962. Objects date from 15,000 B.C. to contemporary times. From ceramics to flint to intricate beadwork, the collection is spectacular. To acquire such a diverse holding Gilcrease purchased both individual objects and entire collections, which in many cases were enormous. His intention was to present the objects in conjunction with art and literary sources in order to properly tell the story of the Americas. Many objects came from private sources. Some were acquired with the aid of Greg Perino, a longtime friend and colleague of Gilcrease, and Dr. David Harner.

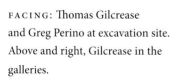

FACING: Thomas Gilcrease and Greg Perino at excavation site. Above and right, Gilcrease in the galleries.

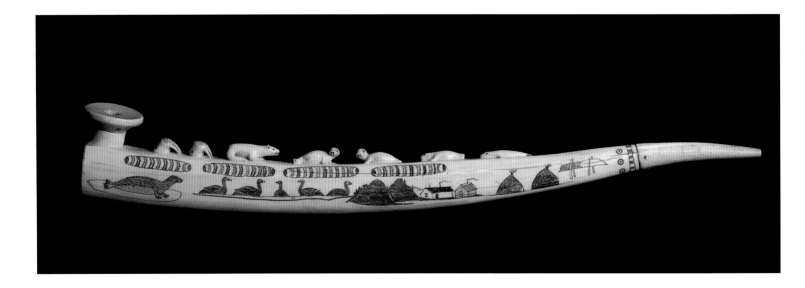

The Frank J. Engles Collection began in Alaska in 1906 and was purchased by the Thomas Gilcrease Foundation in 1950. Containing approximately 1,200 pieces the Engles collection incorporated objects from Alaska and the Pacific Northwest and included stone, jade, ivory and bone. This collection contains many modern and ancient specimens and was an excellent addition to the Gilcrease Museum. Today many of the objects purchased from Engles can be found in the Kravis Discovery Center. Included within the center are ivory pipes made from walrus tusk, ivory combs and knives, several effigies of both animals and humans, and other assorted ivory and bone objects.

The Lloyd Bolles Collection was acquired by Thomas Gilcrease in 1948 and contains nearly 500 objects from the southwestern United States, including materials from both the Anasazi and Mesa Verde peoples. Pottery, beads, and stone points included in the collection remain a valuable research tool for collectors and academics from across the nation. The Bolles Collection was one of the first anthropological groupings acquired by Gilcrease. Its acquisition demonstrated a path toward quickly and effectively enhancing his holdings through the purchase of entire bodies of collections.

The specimen above was a trade item found in the Coronation Gulf of Alaska. The Inuit culture, from which it comes, is one of the few remaining groups that can legally use walrus ivory.

Ivory pipe. Inuit, 19th century. 16 x 3.66 x 1.39. GM 83.1403. ENGLES COLLECTION.

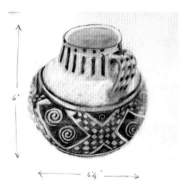

The vessel on the right is from the Kayenta people located in the Four Corners region of the southwestern United States during the Pueblo I-IV periods. In this culture, similar to Mesa Verde, people cultivated beans, corn, and squash and used surplus goods as trade items.

Sketch of an object from the Bolles Collection inventory log.

Jar. 700–1500 A.D. 3.4 x 7. GM 54.3177.

BOLLES COLLECTION.

The Ignacio Bernal Collection, whose acquisition was negotiated during the 1940s and 50s, is a remarkable body of pieces from Mexico. It contains material from several regions and numerous cultures, most notably Aztec and Mayan. Bernal and Gilcrease corresponded over a lengthy period, with Bernal offering particular pieces, illustrated by descriptive photographs, for possible purchase by the Gilcrease Foundation. Today this collection is prized for both its splendor and research potential.

The Mayans inhabited an area in Central America now referred to as the Yucatan Peninsula. The culture traces its origins back nearly 4,000 years. The Classic Period of Mayan Culture was 300—900 A.D. when the jade pendant was produced. The Maya are most noted for their systems of astronomy, including the calendar, mathematics, and writing.

Envelope from Ignacio Bernal addressed to the Thomas Gilcrease Foundation. Included in this envelope were pictures of objects Bernal had for sale. The letter was postmarked 1948.

Human effigy rattle. Mayan, ca. 800 A.D. 8 x 4.83 x 1.99. GM 54.7767. BERNAL COLLECTION.

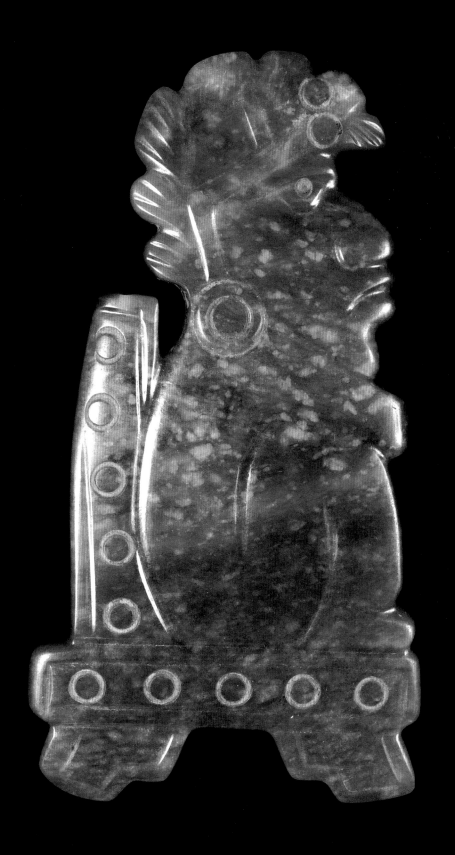

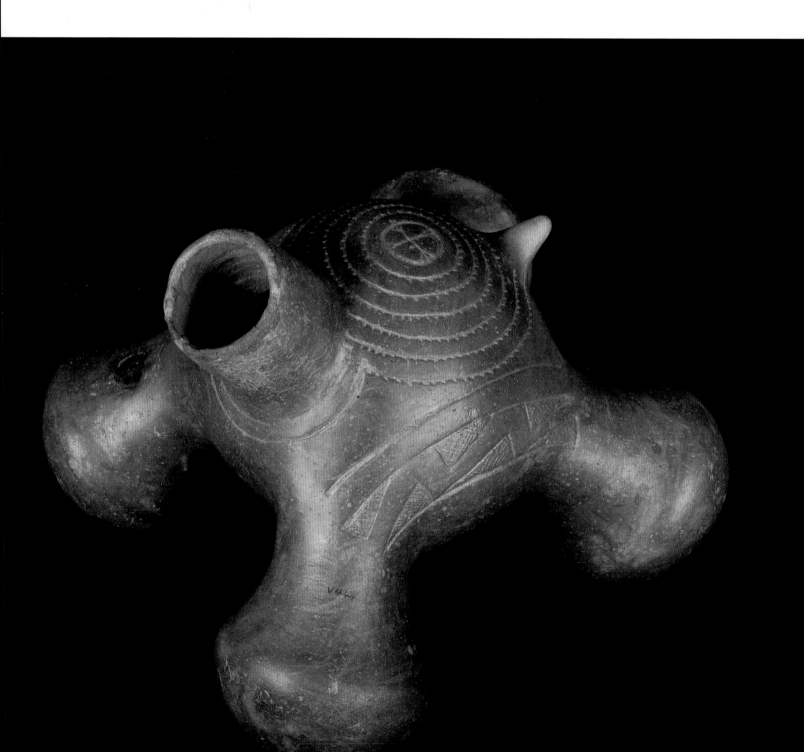

This piece is from the Mississippian period and was created by the Caddo people who occupied territory in Louisiana, eastern Texas, and southern Arkansas. It was found by Lemley in Yell County, Arkansas in the Carden Bottom area.

Ceramic effigy vessel. Caddo, ca. 1600 A.D. 9 x 8.6 x 7.1. GM 54.1651.
LEMLEY COLLECTION.

This ceremonial bifacially thin blade with curved lip was unearthed in Kentucky. Typically ceremonial blades are found in temple mound complexes in the southeastern U.S. and into western Oklahoma.

Blade. Mississippian, 700-1500 A.D. 10.55 x 3.3 x .63. GM 61.1562.
YOUNG COLLECTION.

The Harry J. Lemley Collection, which came to the museum in 1955, contains approximately 50,000 pieces. They are mostly from the Mississippian Era (700 A.D.–1500 A.D.) and were found in Arkansas, Louisiana, and Oklahoma. Gilcrease's own excavations would add to this collection, making it one of the finest groups of Mississippian artifacts in the world and a lively research tool. Lemley lived in Hope, Arkansas, where he was for many years a district judge. The collection, of considerable importance to understanding the mound building cultures in this region, added depth and scale to the anthropological materials at Gilcrease.

The Dr. Hugh Young Collection was one of the last groups of artifacts purchased by Gilcrease before his death. It contains approximately 1,500 archaeological items and was acquired for the institute in 1962. The objects were found in nine different states in the Midwest and South, and include axes, bannerstones, awls, beads, birdstones, copper tools, bracelets, bowls, and two dozen other classifications of objects. Young lived in Nashville, Tennessee, and his collection at the time of acquisition was "purported to be of the finest in existence."

The Willis Tilton Collection is comprised of objects from the Spiro Mound located in Oklahoma. This includes effigies, beads, points, pipes, gorgets, ear spools, axes, blades, and numerous other objects, bringing the total number of items to 934, plus arrows and Moorehead points. Other objects from Spiro Mound loaned to the museum by the University of Tulsa in 1976 complement the collection. Thomas Gilcrease purchased the bulk of the Tilton collection between 1950 and 1959.

These two pieces are large abalone shell masks incised and covered with granular material and inlaid with shells for the eyes. The Chumash inhabited the California coast and several islands just off the coast making them one of the few North American peoples to regularly make trips into the sea.

Mask. Chumash. (front and back views) 9 x 6.5. GM 90.1470. TILTON COLLECTION.

FACING: Mask. Chumash. 9 x 6.5. GM 90.1468. TILTON COLLECTION.

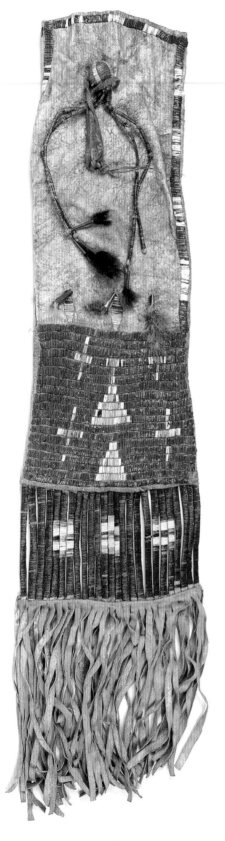

The Emil Lenders Collection is a remarkable assortment of Plains Indians objects from the 19th and 20th centuries, including items from the Osage, Kiowa, Comanche, Southern Cheyenne, Blackfoot, Lakota, Dakota, Winnebago, Oto, and Ponca tribes. Acquired by Gilcrease in 1950 the objects have remained available for research and been displayed repeatedly throughout the years. Emil Lenders was an artist and collector of western American culture and influences. The collection he amassed contains approximately 600 objects.

The Joseph Henry Sharp Collection, acquired by Gilcrease by 1962, contains nearly 70 pieces once located in Sharp's studio. These include many southwestern and Plains Indians objects. It also includes letters between Gilcrease and Sharp about the nature of specific items and their authenticity. Most notable is a letter discussing two Peruvian textiles and how Sharp had acquired them.

Quilled pipe bag with leather fringe and a quilled ball at the top. It is decorated with dyed feathers, metal cones, and glass beads. Pipe bags were created to hold sacred items and secured with a drawstring at the top.

Quilled Pipe Bag. Sioux, late 19th century. 31 x 7. GM 84.577. LENDERS COLLECTION.

Envelope and Letter from Joseph Henry Sharp to Gilcrease regarding the authenticity of items Gilcrease was hoping to acquire.

FACING: Chief's blanket, detail. Navajo, ca. 1880. 41 x 56.625. GM 97.47.

War bonnets began as a northern Plains tradition in the early 1800s. Bonnets are made with eagle feathers and include a beaded band across the front. Typically, the beaded band is the first indicator of which tribe made the bonnet; tribes varied in the designs they favored.

FACING: War bonnet. Sioux, 19th century. GM 54.247. LENDERS COLLECTION.

After the European immigration into America, glass beads began to replace porcupine quills as the primary decorative motifs for leather objects. Generally they were easier to work with and were inexpensive to acquire. These moccasins were made for a Cheyenne man.

Moccasins. Cheyenne, 19th century. 10.5 x 3.62. GM 84.387a,b. J. H. SHARP COLLECTION.

Thomas Gilcrease, Nelson Glueck,
and Alfred Aaronson.

FACING: Gilcrease Museum interior.

Above left, Gilcrease and Tom Denney at Klunk Mound 11. Right, Gilcrease and David Harner at Hopewell Mounds in Illinois, 1960.

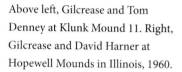

Platform pipes were created by the Hopewell people of the Bedford Mounds, Illinois, area around 200 A.D. The body of this one is made from black steatite and the anejo is posed in a fighting position. The eyes are made of river pearls and the teeth are carved from a real beaver tooth. This object is one of a kind and is reported to be the finest Hopewell pipe in existence.

FACING: Beaver effigy pipe. Woodland Period. GM 61.1140. GREG PERINO COLLECTION.

Greg Perino, a founding member of the Illinois State Archaeological Society, was employed by Gilcrease in 1955. Perino's job was to manage the anthropology collection at the museum and to lead excavations carried out by Gilcrease in his later years. The first of these digs was located north of St. Louis, Missouri, where several Hopewell mounds had been discovered. Perino was known for his ability to select sites and over the years he would develop a great many tools that are still employed today in excavating. The objects acquired by Gilcrease in collaboration with Perino, still referred to at the museum as the Perino Collection, came mainly from the Hopewellian and Mississippian eras. Dr. David Harner was the third man in the Gilcrease-Perino-Harner excavating team.

Harner was a remarkable man. Originally from Oklahoma but living in Springdale, Arkansas, he met Gilcrease while touring the museum one Sunday afternoon. During that chance meeting Dr. Harner struck up a conversation with Gilcrease about whether or not certain items Gilcrease was about to purchase were fakes. He concluded they were. From that point on the two men remained friends. Harner began going on digs with Perino and Gilcrease at his own expense. Between 1955 and 1962 the three men made numerous trips throughout the Midwest in search of prehistoric items. In the year of his death Gilcrease was planning an excavation in Mexico, and it has been said that if he had had the money and ultimately the time he would have ventured into Egypt and Greece.

Thomas Gilcrease's legacy preserves the history of Native American peoples for posterity. Without his desire to accumulate these objects, many would perhaps have been lost. Since his death the museum has acquired through both gifts and purchases many important pieces which have continued to add to the depth of the collection.

Mak-hos-kah, chief
(White Cloud.)

Masterworks of a Master Collector

ANNE MORAND, CHIEF CURATOR, C.M. RUSSELL MUSEUM

Gilcrease galleries, early 1950s.

Mak-hos-kah, 1825. Charles Bird King. 31.375 x 17, oil/wood, GM 0126.1198.

THE 1940S FOR THOMAS GILCREASE marked the devotion of energies to his fine art acquisitions as never before. An examination of highlights among his hundreds of art acquisitions during the 1940s and 1950s reveals an opportunistic rather than systematic approach—he bought things he liked when they came to his attention. New York dealers and galleries came to know about Thomas Gilcrease and his interest in American art. He often purchased paintings during visits to see art in their sales rooms, but the gallery owners who listened and paid attention soon began to seek out things they felt would appeal to Gilcrease, and notified him. Gilcrease was a demanding patron, but had the money to back up his demands, especially in an era when there were few collectors of his caliber who were seeking American fine art.

Gilcrease bought Charles Bird King's *Mak-hos-kah, Chief of the Goways (White Cloud)* on February 1, 1944 from the Macbeth Gallery. Founded by William Macbeth in 1892 it was the first New York gallery to solely handle American art. Four years later, on July 30, 1946, he acquired a portrait of Cherokee chief, *Cunne Shote* by English painter Francis Parsons from another New York dealer James P. Labey. The portrait was painted in London in 1762 during the visit by Cunne Shote and two other Cherokee chiefs to King George III.

The day after Christmas 1946, Gilcrease bought the first of two large paintings by Henry Farny from the Schneider-Gabriel Galleries in New York, *Fording the Stream*. A few months later, on March 11, 1947, Gilcrease added *The Sorceror*. These two American Indian subjects fit well with Gilcrease's acquisition of the Philip Cole collection of western art that was purchased in 1944 and delivered in 1947.

Even though it signaled the close of his San Antonio museum and the move to Tulsa, 1947 was a banner year for Thomas Gilcrease as he purchased several important groups of artworks that expanded upon his existing collections. From dealer C. Bland Jamison he obtained a set of sixteen exquisite watercolors painted by Thomas Moran after his trip to Yellowstone in 1871. The set, including *The Grand Canyon of the Yellowstone*, was commissioned in 1872 by Sir William Blackmore and commemorated the English nobleman's visit to the area.

Fording the Stream, 1905. Henry Farny. 29.5 x 40.375, oil/canvas, GM 0127.1224.

The Grand Canyon of the Yellowstone, 1872. Thomas Moran. 26.5 x 21.5, watercolor/paper, GM 0226.1619.

His-oo-san-chees, the Little Spaniard, 1836. George Catlin. 19.375 x 14.5, watercolor/paper, GM 0226.1534.

Through London dealer William Robinson Ltd. Gilcrease acquired hundreds of artworks and papers by George Catlin from the heirs of collector Sir Thomas Phillipps. With paintings such as *Indian Council (Sioux)* the collection represented the artist's work and extensive travels in the American West during the 1830s and his subsequent promotion of that work in England. While in London Catlin sold his collection to Phillipps in order to pay debts. The Phillipps collection meshed well with Gilcrease's previous purchases of Catlins such as watercolor portrait *His-oo-san-chees, the Little Spaniard,* from Kennedy Galleries on November 1, 1940.

Indian Council (Sioux), 1847. George Catlin. 29.75 x 36.25, oil/canvas, GM 0176.2170.

One of Gilcrease's most valued sources was M. Knoedler & Co. in New York. Knoedler had been established 100 years earlier and had a reputation for handling some of the best American art. In 1947 Gilcrease, with Knoedler, began the systematic, multi-year acquisition of more than a hundred works by Alfred Jacob Miller from various heirs. Again Gilcrease was adding to works he had purchased earlier from Kennedy Galleries, such as three watercolors on October 23, 1942. The collection would eventually include studio oils like *Sir William Drummond Stewart Meeting Indian Chief* that was painted in Baltimore, as well as oil and watercolor

Sir William Drummond Stewart Meeting Indian Chief. Alfred Jacob Miller. 37.5 x 46.5, oil/canvas, GM 0126.738.

sketches painted while Miller was expedition artist with Stewart's entourage to the West in 1837. During 1947, Gilcrease also purchased some noteworthy single pieces from Knoedler, including one of the most important paintings in the art collection, Thomas Eakins's landmark portrait of Zuni ethnologist Frank Hamilton Cushing. Inconceivably deaccessioned by the original owner, the Brooklyn Museum, the portrait was sold to Gilcrease on February 25, 1947.

Although the majority of Gilcrease's art came through New York galleries, he did work with regional dealers. From the hundred-year-old McCaughen and Burr Gallery in St. Louis came Emanuel Leutze's *Westward the Empire Takes Its Way*. The first study for Leutze's heroic-sized mural in the U. S. Capitol, it was made in Leutze's St. Louis studio in 1861. It is not clear whether Gilcrease was in St. Louis when the purchase was made on September 17, 1947, but a few days later Gilcrease was working once again with Knoedler in New York. On September 22, he purchased one of the most poignant paintings to enter his collection, George De Forest Brush's *Mourning Her Brave*. Based on Brush's observations in the West in the 1880s, this compelling image of grief, based on a Crow woman's loss, is universal in its appeal.

Frank Hamilton Cushing, 1895. Thomas Eakins. 90 x 60, oil/canvas, GM 0126.2315.

FACING: *Mourning Her Brave,* detail, 1883. George De Forest Brush. 45.375 x 35.375, oil/panel, GM 0126.1189.

The next year Gilcrease enlarged upon his earlier Thomas Moran acquisition from Knoedler by purchasing the artist's estate September 30, 1948. Held in trust by Moran's daughter Ruth until her death, the collection included more than 2,000 paintings, watercolors, drawings, original prints, letters, and other personal papers Ranging from enormous oils such as *Shoshone Falls on the Snake River, Idaho* to tiny, quickly executed field sketches, the collection represented the entire span of Moran's life, career, and travels. Knoedler knew that the artist's desire to have the collection remain intact would be honored by a collector like Gilcrease.

As remarkable as it was, the September 30 sale from Knoedler included items in addition to the Moran estate. Along with twenty-five more Miller watercolors and oils, Gilcrease received John James Audubon's *The Wild Turkey*. Painted in 1845, it is the largest of the oils based on Audubon's study of bird species in America. Although Audubon painted and sold other oils to support his publication *Birds of America,* he kept *The Wild Turkey* in his personal collection.

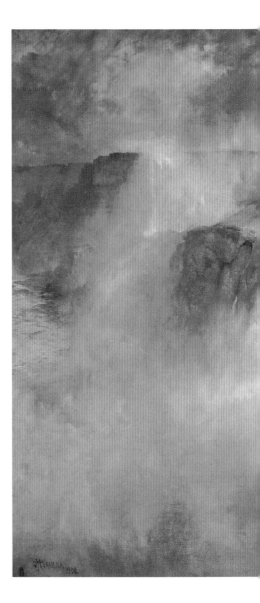

The Wild Turkey, 1845. John James Audubon. 53.25 x 40.5, oil/canvas, GM 0126.2322.

Shoshone Falls on the Snake River, 1900. Thomas Moran. 71 x 144.5, oil/canvas, GM 0126.2339.

Black Hawk and His Son, Whirling Thunder, 1833. John Wesley Jarvis. 29.625 x 36, oil/canvas, GM 0126.1007.

FACING: *Sierra Nevada Morning,* 1870. Albert Bierstadt. 71 x 101, oil/canvas, GM 0126.2305; Gilcrease gallery in the 1950s.

Gilcrease was busy in 1949 completing the construction of his museum in Tulsa, but he found time to purchase a work that became a signature piece for his collection, *Black Hawk and His Son, Whirling Thunder* by John Wesley Jarvis. Knoedler sold Gilcrease the stunning double portrait of the Sauk and Fox leaders on March 30, 1949.

Gilcrease did not slow down as he entered the 1950s. Just three days into the new decade, he acquired John Vanderlyn's *Washington and Lafayette at the Battle of Brandywine* from Knoedler, the first of several works that continued his interest in early American art and added depth to his collections. Less than a month later, he purchased Albert Bierstadt's sublime *Sierra Nevada Morning* from

Portrait of John Rowe, 1748.
Robert Feke. 36 x 29, oil/canvas,
GM 0126.1003.

*Portrait of Mrs. John Apthorp, née
Hannah Greenleaf.* 1765. John
Singleton Copley. 38 x 33.5,
oil/canvas, GM 0126.1012.

Kennedy Galleries on February 1, 1950. The acquisition of these paintings, it turns
out, was just a prelude to his stunning purchase from Knoedler on April 19, 1950,
which included colonial portraits, unusual in a collection as far west as Oklahoma.
John Smibert's *Portrait of John Cotton,* Robert Feke's *Portrait of John Rowe,* and John
Singleton Copley's *Portrait of Mrs. John Apthorp,* all painted in the 1700s, represent
the earliest known painters of note working in America.

Charles Carroll of Carrollton.
Thomas Sully. 96.75 x 67.25,
oil/canvas, GM 0126.1019.

James Madison, ca. 1792. Charles
Willson Peale. 36.25 x 31.5,
oil/canvas, GM 0126.1006.

But the April 19 purchase consisted of even more, such as Thomas Sully's portrait of Charles Carroll of Carrollton, the oldest living signer of the Declaration of Independence, George G. A. Healy's portrait of Stephen Douglas, the great Lincoln debater, and Winslow Homer's *Watching the Breakers,* a seascape painted on the Maine coast. The Homer is an oddity among this group not only for its subject, but also for its provenance. The portraits had descended down through family members. The Homer was deaccessioned from the Art Institute of Chicago.

Over the next few years, Gilcrease added to his Western collections with paintings such as John Mix Stanley's *The Buffalo Hunt.* Purchased from Knoedler on February 9, 1952, the painting had hung in Millard Fillmore's White House. As with the Catlin and Miller collections, Gilcrease was particularly interested in eye-witness accounts of the 19th-century West. Stanley had traveled in the West as an expeditionary artist.

For reasons discussed elsewhere in this book, Gilcrease sold his collection to the city of Tulsa in 1955 and it became the nucleus of what was popularly called Gilcrease Museum. But he was still acquiring art even as the transfer of ownership was taking place. In January he purchased an extraordinary work from Knoedler, James McNeil Whistler's *Nocturne, the Solent,* and it went to the city along with the majority of his collection. Serene and cool, this seascape off the coast of Chile by the American expatriot represented an understanding by Gilcrease that there were certain critical artists that should be included in the collection. Gilcrease had to stretch, though, for Whistler's work primarily focused on European subjects.

Watching the Breakers, 1891.
Winslow Homer. 37 x 47,
oil/canvas, GM 0126.2264.

OVERLEAF: *Nocturne, the Solent,*
1866. James McNeill Whistler. 30.25
x 46.5, oil/canvas, GM 0176.1185.

The Buffalo Hunt. John Mix Stanley. 35.125 x 46, oil/canvas, GM 0126.1146.

FACING: *Siouxs Playing Ball.* Charles Deas. 41.25 x 47.875, oil/canvas, GM 0126.1152.

After 1955, Gilcrease continued to collect artworks, most of which were given to the museum after his death by the Thomas Gilcrease Foundation. The post-1955 acquisitions were approached with the same vigor and keen eye that characterized his earlier choices. On March 18, 1957, New York dealer Victor Spark sold him three very diverse subjects. Charles Deas's *Siouxs Playing Ball* is a romantic interpretation of a Native American stickball competition painted during the artist's time in the West in the 1840s. Jasper Cropsey's *View On Lake George* represents the tamed wilderness of upstate New York in 1874. And John Singer Sargent's dynamic *Arrival of American Troops at the Front* was painted on site in France in 1918.

Penn's Treaty with the Indians, 1809.
Benjamin West. 74 x 107.5,
oil/canvas, GM 0126.1021

On November 11, 1958 Knoedler once again came through with paintings by Charles Willson Peale and Benjamin West that seriously enriched the already priceless collection. Peale's incomparable portrait of James Madison was painted for the artist's own museum in Philadelphia fifteen years before Madison was elected president of the United States. West's heroic-sized *Penn's Treaty with the Indians* was unfinished at the time of the artist's death, and a duplicate of the earlier version at the Pennsylvania Academy of the Fine Arts. Also part of this acquisition were *The Portrait of Red Jacket* by John Neagle and several large Catlin Indian scenes.

Gilcrease was able to add significance to an earlier acquisition by purchasing on January 6, 1959 the portrait of Syacust Ukah, another of the three Cherokee chiefs who had gone to England in 1762. In doing so he gained a representative piece by England's greatest portraitist, Sir Joshua Reynolds. The portrait came through Knoedler, who in the same sale provided John Trumbull's *Portrait of Charles Wilkes* and Ralph Earl's portrait of Matthew Clarkson. Now Gilcrease had something by nearly all the important painters of the period.

This exceedingly abbreviated review of Thomas Gilcrease's activity as a collector demonstrates both his range and dedication. With artworks that span 400 years, Gilcrease developed a collection that effectively serves as a survey of the history of American art. His devotion to seeking out the best that could be obtained is evident in the quality of individual pieces that continue to be recognized as masterworks. To his credit, Gilcrease also understood the benefit of extensive collections by single artists, an idea that drove him to secure the outstanding assemblage of works by Catlin, Miller, and Moran. With these three examples alone, Gilcrease added immeasurably to the art historical appreciation and understanding of the artists. His farsightedness in creating the collection and an institution to house it extends beyond the physical boundaries of the museum and his own temporal boundary.

BILLBOARD SIGN

PUBLIC SCHOOL TOUR

ART STORAGE AREA

Thomas Gilcrease with his two sons, Thomas Gilcrease Jr. and Barton, 1958. Des Cygne Gilcrease (1929–1968), daughter of Thomas Gilcrease and Norma Smallwood.

EVEN AFTER OWNERSHIP OF HIS HOLDINGS had been transferred to the city of Tulsa, Thomas Gilcrease continued to spend much of his time and remaining fortune adding significant art and artifacts to that collection which still bears the Gilcrease family name. In his lifetime, he had acquired hundreds of thousands of historical objects—rare artifacts, documents, books, maps, manuscripts, and works of fine art. He had been a successful farmer and rancher. He had been an oil producer and banker. For a time, he had raised horses, cattle, and three children. He had married twice and traveled the world. He had pursued life with an unquenchable passion for learning. He had developed and maintained an appreciation for history that would shape his perspective on all things. Ultimately, the life of Thomas Gilcrease had been made up of an enduring desire to leave behind him something worthwhile, "a track," as he often called it. It was a life made up of hard work and disappointment, but also of wonder. Today, his track continues to be seen in many forms. It remains a broad set of imprints that can perhaps never be fully appreciated or understood.

Beginning in the early 1930s, Gilcrease worked to build not only an art museum but also a library that would be a repository of great books and historical documents. The establishment of the Thomas Gilcrease Institute of American History and Art in Tulsa in 1949 was the culmination of his long dream. To him, history and art were fundamentally intertwined. Regardless of fame, notoriety, or estimation in the realm of artistic merit, works of fine art could be also be appreciated very much like documents—they could be seen as records of the past, of the times in which they were conceived and executed. Indeed, the vast collection of artworks compiled by Thomas Gilcrease would eventually become an important archive in the study of American history and culture. They would become a fundamental source for research, particularly in areas related to the understanding of Native American custom and traditional life.

For Gilcrease, the past was a preeminent force upon current circumstances. It informed and shaped much of contemporary life. To him, history was well more than an introduction to the present. It was an essential distillation of the thoughts, hopes, and dreams of individuals and cultures that had come before. An understanding of history was essential to fully apprehending not only the present but beyond. It was as much a predictor of future events as it was a record of past occurrences. In a tribute to his good friend Robert Humber wrote that, for Thomas Gilcrease, "History was not only a grand prologue to the present but an instrument for programming the future. He would have agreed with Edmund Burke that history was a contract between the living and the dead—but he would have added that the irrevocable, bona fide provision of the contract was that each generation would make the world a better place in which to live."

Thomas Gilcrease at Pont de Gar. At left, fishing.

Shortly before the death of Thomas Gilcrease, plans were approved for the expansion of the museum. Unfortunately, Gilcrease did not live to see it completed. Below, proposed addition to the museum.

FACING: Gilcrease under construction, bottom, and an artist's rendering of completed museum. GM 4327.3061.

PROPOSED ADDITION TO GILCREASE MUSEUM

TULSA — OKLAHOMA

JOS. R KOBERLING AIA ARCHITECT

Scenes from a life: Clockwise from far left, Gilcrease in 1944; receiving an honorary degree; with his daughter Des Cygne in front of the portrait by Charles Banks Wilson; at the groundbreaking for the museum expansion; made an honorary member of the Sioux Nation in 1946. On his left is George Whirlwind Soldier and on the right, Henry Standing Bear.

As Humber noted, the time of Thomas Gilcrease was "the natal day of great museums." Around the world, vast wealth was being spent amassing vast collections. Museums and libraries were being "founded by men and women of extraordinary vision, astounding vigor and unselfish dedication. There seemed to be no limit to their aspirations…They acted as though they were simply the custodians of their time…" For Gilcrease, to be the "custodian" of American history through collection-building was a fundamental life enterprise that satisfied a deeply-rooted need "to accomplish something significant." "It was an unconscious and ever-present goal," said Humber. "He never considered himself a great man—not even an unusual man—but simply a human being who…might produce a work worthy to be remembered…"

When he passed ownership of his collection to the city of Tulsa in 1955, Gilcrease knew that he had been merely a caretaker. In his hands had been tangible evidence of the American past, yet he knew that any historical record was

Gilcrease in Jackson, Wyoming, 1956. Above, in a sombrero at a theme party.

FACING: Top, at Mont Brevent, France, and at Artist's Point, Washington.

far too broad to ever be fully compiled. He had held letters by Benjamin Franklin, Thomas Jefferson, and Andrew Jackson. He had collected and prized the writings of Diego Columbus, Hernan Cortez, Diego de Trujillo, and Father Kino—among the earliest chroniclers of life in the western hemisphere. He had owned the *Codex Canadiensis* and a manuscript copy of the Declaration of Independence. He had accumulated a significant collection of precolumbian artifacts, many of which he had personally helped to unearth. He had owned a vast number of paintings and sculpture that remain among the finest of their genres ever composed. The collection was his life's effort, compiled with an awareness of the diversity of culture—of the complexities of national and regional identity—comprised across time and space in an attempt to influence contemporary life.

Thomas Gilcrease's deep fondness for the collection and his strong desire for keeping it intact was witnessed by friend and artist Charles Banks Wilson who recalled an encounter between Gilcrease and Amon Carter, rival collector and eventual fellow museum founder. In Gilcrease's Tulsa office, Carter made an audacious and unexpected offer for the purchase of works by Charles M. Russell in the Gilcrease collection. Taking a blank check from his pocket, the Texan signed it and slowly pushed it across the Oklahoman's desk. According to Wilson, Gilcrease merely raised a wry eyebrow and said, "Now, Mr. Carter, if someone asked you to sell one of your children, would you do it?"

The collection maintained a value to Gilcrease well beyond any pecuniary worth. In his later years, he would spend much of his time in the halls and galleries of the museum, contemplating the treasures he had amassed alongside a growing number of visitors. He enjoyed watching the collection's admirers with a quiet sense of accomplishment. He knew that he had built something worthwhile that transcended the great sum of his time, labor, and fortune. Each specimen of art and historical artifact had a unique value to him. Through them, he communed with worlds long since passed, with people long gone but who would now be remembered for all time.

Thomas Gilcrease died on May 5, 1962 of a sudden stroke. On his quiet perch overlooking the city of Tulsa, his last days were in the spring when all of life was blooming around him. The flowers, shrubs, and bushes of his gardens were alive with a subtle brilliance. Songbirds sang with a gentle yet keen intensity. In his seventy-second year, Thomas Gilcrease died among the natural things that he loved. From his days as a young man in Indian Territory to later his jaunting about the Jardin du Trocadero in Paris, nature and gardens had been a passion and he had long loved growing things. He had spent the past several years improving the grounds of the

Gilcrease estate. For all his travels, the southern crest of the Osage Hills had remained a place of simple yet profound pleasure. At the end of his life, it had become not so much a refuge as a place to exercise an artistic ability of his own. While he had spent time traveling, designing his gardens, and organizing archaeological excavations, his last days were also devoted to pursuits that significantly enhanced the collection he had started decades before.

Gilcrease at Artist's Point, Washington, above, and at Mont Blanc, lower left.

FACING: Gilcrease on the front porch of his house on the grounds of Gilcrease Museum in 1958. The modest stone structure had been home to Gilcrease and his second bride, an art storage area and gallery, and for a brief period an orphanage. In the end it was the place the philanthropist, collector, and oilman spent his last days.

According to his wishes, Thomas Gilcrease's funeral was held on the museum grounds, not far from his eventual resting place on the slope at the foot of the Gilcrease home. Services for the Oklahoma oilman and philanthropist were performed amid a gathering of family, friends, admirers, business acquaintances, and members of the press. His long list of accomplishments was recited. There were prayers and thoughtful wishes. A small contingent of Native Americans in Plains Indian dress performed solemnly. His longtime friend Wolf Robe Hunt raised a bow and arrow, aimed toward the heavens, and launched a single arrow to the western sky to signify a great man's passing into another realm.

In a last gift to the museum, Thomas Gilcrease bequeathed land and priceless works of art. To the people of Tulsa, he gave his home and beloved estate. He gave significant paintings that have since been called "Gilcrease Treasures." In the world of art and its knowing admirers, among historians and interpreters of the past, Thomas Gilcrease left a bounty that has yet to be fully comprehended. He gave to the people not only a collection but also a way of looking at their own heritage.

The legacy of Thomas Gilcrease remains fluid. It is a thing that perhaps can never be fully realized. The museum that still bears his name remains more than a grand repository of objects. It is more than a mere storehouse of relics, writings, and objets d'art set aside to maintain and commemorate the linkages of cultural memory. Indeed, the Gilcrease Museum collection is more significantly a representation of contemporary times. Its long-term care and preservation is a marker not only of the past but also of the present, of what is valued by society. The legacy of Thomas Gilcrease will forever continue to speak to our collective imagination. It will inform our interpretation and appreciation of those who have come before us and their times. As we honor them, we also honor ourselves and subsequent generations. Thomas Gilcrease's national treasure remains a living thing that will long shape our notions of history and American life.

Gilcrease's funeral, 1962.

FACING: Wolf Robe Hunt shoots an arrow into the sky in honor of his friend.

The mausoleum of Thomas Gilcrease, on the grounds of Gilcrease Museum.